W9-BDA-871

HOMAGE TO OCEANIA

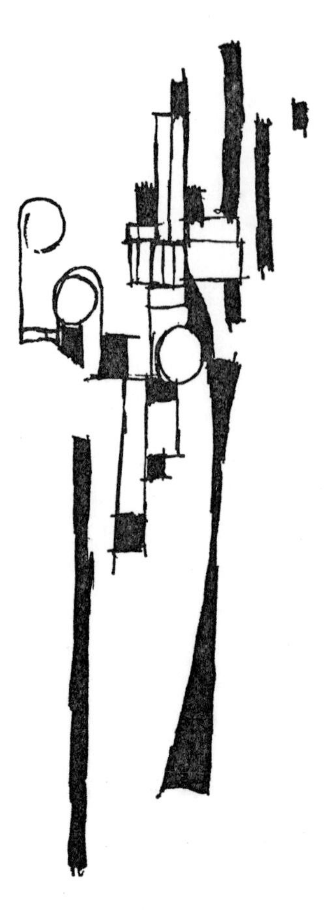

Then everything includes itself in power,
Power into will, will into appetite;
And appetite, an universal wolf,
So doubly seconded with will and power,
Must make perforce an universal prey,
And last eat up himself.

Ulysses in Shakespeare's
"Troilus and Cressida," I, iii

Homage to Oceania

The Prophetic Vision of George Orwell

RUTH ANN LIEF

Ohio State University Press

Library of Congress Catalogue Card Number: 68–28811

DEDICATED TO LEN

PREFACE

Perhaps what most strikes one who reads or rereads the work of George Orwell today is the continuing relevance of his governing concepts to a world which has changed markedly since his death. The particular events and circumstances from which these concepts derive are dated, as political events and sociological circumstances inevitably are. But the ideas and ideals explicit in Orwell's critical and historical writing and implicit in his fiction live in the heritage of free men as vigorously now as when they informed Orwell's thought and directed his energies. The effect of automation, the alienation of modern man from his fellow men, from history, and from the natural beauty of his earth, and certainly the emergence of totalitarianism as a seemingly invincible alternative to political vitality and responsibility—these questions are peculiarly of the twentieth century, and one does not foresee adequate answers by the end of the century. By addressing himself to these questions, Orwell is still very much a man for our season.

These questions, however, led Orwell not to formulate abstractions even less manageable than automation, alienation, and totalitarianism but to consider how man could earn his bread with dignity, spend his leisure free from anxiety, and die with the conviction that the world would continue with hope for the unborn. These, of course, are eternal questions, and because Orwell approached them as a man rather than as a specialist, it seems likely he will be good for more than one season.

My interest in Orwell in the following pages is neither biographical nor literary. He had no genius either for living or for artistic creation. He was remarkable for political passion and insight and, fortunately for posterity, he was remarkably articulate. His works preserve a record of one man's deep and persistent concern for the world which, by rights, belongs to all men. To that concern my own homage is paid.

In addition my homage is due not only to friends and family members who encouraged my study but specifically to David Freeman Hawke, Professor of History at Pace College, who read the manuscript when he had more important things to do. For his friendly prodding and professional attention I can find no adequate thanks. I am indebted to another friend, Professor James Light of the University of Bridgeport, whose early interest in my work caused it to be read sympathetically by Professor Walter D. Love, then managing editor of Studies in British History and Culture at the University of Bridgeport. Although Professor Love's efforts on behalf of the manuscript were cut short by his early and tragic death, his belief in it sustained me through a period of many doubts. His successor, Professor Christopher Collier, also of the University of Bridgeport, generously urged me to find a publisher and helped me to that end. Finally, I am proud to acknowledge my gratitude to Professor Richard D. Altick of Ohio State University. Had it not been for his disinterested sponsorship and good offices, all this homage might never have become a matter of public record.

Ruth Ann Lief

Contents

HOMAGE TO OCEANIA

CHAPTER ONE

THE ARTIST AND THE HANGMAN: THE SUBJECTIVE TRUTH AND THE OFFICIAL LIE

What a writer, in the way of confession or clarification, says of his motives for writing and his purposes in particular works perhaps matters little except to curiosity-seekers. Robinson Jeffers, who was clearly a poet but who has been miscalled many things, inclined briefly to his critics and declared, in verse, that he could "tell lies in prose." George Orwell may have had a similar flash of cynicism when he declared, in fiction, "it *is* fun when you have good food and good wine inside you—to demonstrate that we live in a dead and rotting world." [1] But Orwell was too honest to be cynical of motives he made a matter of public record, as he did in an essay entitled bluntly "Why I Write":

1) "sheer egoism": an attempt perhaps to secure "personal immortality" in an age of disbelief, a quest which he names in "Looking Back on the Spanish War" as "the major problem of our time."

2) "esthetic enthusiasm": which he evinces, for example, in his tribute to Kipling's verse: "A good bad poem is a graceful monument to the obvious."

3) "historical impulse": the desire "to see things as they are, to find out true facts and store them up for the use of posterity."

4) "political purpose": to "push the world in a certain direction, to alter other people's ideas of the kind of society that they should strive after."

Orwell's assurance that the first three motives "outweigh the fourth" seems to conflict with assertions he made in this essay and in others:

> . . . no book is genuinely free from political bias. The opinion that art should have nothing to do with politics is itself a political attitude.[2]
>
> . . . every writer, especially every novelist, *has* a "message". . . . All art is propaganda.[3]
>
> In our age there is no such thing as "keeping out of politics." All issues are political issues. . . .[4]

He insisted that because they "leave their mark even on the smallest detail of his work," a writer's "political and religious beliefs are not excrescences to be laughed away." [5] His own "lifeless books . . . purple passages, sentences without meaning, decorative adjectives and humbug generally" he attributes to lack of political purpose and declares, "Every line of serious work that I have written since 1936 has been written, directly or indirectly, *against* totalitarianism and *for* democratic socialism, as I understand it." [6]

Orwell's two most intensely political novels are, without doubt, his most distinguished; without them, his fame today might be modest, if not obscure. His ideal from the beginning was to do what he did "with full consciousness" in *Animal Farm:* "to fuse political purpose and artistic purpose into a whole."

Not only as a novelist but, understandably, as a critic, Orwell refused to approach art simply for art's sake, but his critical essays show that it cost him a struggle to remain convinced that art was handmaiden to something more important than itself. Like writers in other times who evolved elaborate justifications for a profession so patently pleasurable and sedentary as to seem frivolous in the eyes of the world, Orwell was conscience-stricken for himself, for anyone who sat aside from the current of events and pushed a pen. Surrounded not only by the age-old iniquities and inequities of the human condition but by terrors peculiar to an age that has the secret of total power, he did not entirely trust the pen to be mightier than the sword. The triumph of totalitarianisms meant the disappearance of certain old assumptions—among them the assumption that evil defeats itself in the long run and good triumphs, the assumption, in fact, that good and evil can even be distinguished. Evil could be vanquished neither by itself—since it had finally found the secret of eternal life—nor by novelists but only by a military force commensurate to it.[7] The "invasion of literature by politics" was bound to seem to Orwell a phenomenon peculiar to his generation, a generation forced by its environment to make a protective adaptation, to enlarge its conscience at the expense of faculties less suited to survival:

> we have developed a sort of compunction which our grandparents did not have, an awareness of the enormous injustice and misery of the world, and a guilt-stricken feeling that one ought to be doing something about it, which makes a purely esthetic attitude towards life impossible. No one, now, could devote himself to literature as single-mindedly as Joyce or Henry James.[8]

For Orwell, certainly, political commitment was a deeply moral matter in an age of superstates embodying "evil." After his experience in the Spanish war—from 1936 onwards—Orwell may have suspected that it was already too late to stop ideological movements which were unhampered by a respect for current or historical fact, let alone a respect for human life. But, like any dedicated fighter, he believed one should try to stop them by *all means,* whether the means were military or intellectual. In an all-out struggle, art could not be regarded as an end in itself but as one means toward a desirable end.

Fiction and poetry, however, are notoriously non-utilitarian, even when they are written by men of strong political convictions. That propagandists use them as means to an end does not alter their essential nature. The artists admired by the Nazis may have been temporarily discredited in the eyes of anti-Nazis during the second world war, but the Allied cause did not suffer materially by having literary and musical antagonists in the libraries and concert halls of Germany. It is misleading even to say that the Nazis misused works of art. Short of being used as wrapping paper or as fuel, a novel or a painting has no practical value. What it does have transcends ideological squabbles and is affected by them only if, in the course of conflict or as a result of official policy, the work of art is destroyed completely.

Unlike works of art, propaganda has *only* practical value. It is used up ceaselessly as a means to an end and is never preserved for its own sake. The writing which interested Orwell, even when it was good *bad* writing, was not propaganda; and, although the distinction between art and propaganda is blurred in some of his shocking and quotable pronouncements, Orwell's criticism shows that he did know the difference between them, however much he denied the existence of objective criteria. To the end of his life he maintained that literary judgments, at best, rested on "trumped-up" reasons for irrational preferences. The most he would admit was a difference between a "literary" and a "non-literary" reaction to a book. "I like this book," he cautiously declares in "Writers and Leviathan," is not "a non-literary reaction":

> the non-literary reaction is "This book is on my side, and therefore I must discover merits in it." Of course, when one praises a book for political reasons one may be emotionally sincere, in . . . that one does feel strong approval of it, but also it often happens that party solidarity demands a plain lie.[9]

Orwell promptly enough gave the lie to the guardians of British solidarity who in 1945 were hanging P. G. Wodehouse in verbal effigy for his broadcasts in collaboration with the Germans, and who were getting ready to burn his novels on the assumption that their author must have been a traitor all along. In this case, Orwell goes to work, as a critic should, to examine the evidence. He finds it inconceivable, from a study of Wodehouse's novels, that their author ever imagined problems more complex than those faced by boys in public schools and their fathers in private clubs. Wodehouse was simply a political innocent, and his fiction, far from showing treasonable tendencies, was an anachronism of peculiarly English stamp. The characters in this fiction might be fools or cads, but their notions of superiority did not exempt them —as comparable notions exempted the Nazis—from the consequences of their deeds. Had Wodehouse been a really effective propagandist for supermen, modern or old-fashioned, Orwell might have found it harder to forgive him; but it was clear to Orwell that a man whose political development had been arrested in the "Edwardian age" could hardly be taken seriously as a traitor to England in the 1940's. The public hangmen might be sincere enough in their strong feelings of disapproval, but their attempt to incriminate Wodehouse on the basis of his fiction was nothing but "humbug," however sincere.[10]

Modern war, to be sure, was no game of cricket, and Orwell was far less tolerant of what he considered fascist tendencies in writers who, whether or not they had a chance to use German radio facilities, deprecated and feared the "human equality" cherished by freedom-loving men. Writing of William Butler Yeats, Orwell tasks the Marxist critics for not having established the connection between an author's politics and his style. Impatient with Yeats' mysticism, which he sees as a cowardly excuse for denying the possibility of progress, and sensing that Yeats was a "great hater of democracy," Orwell sets out to hang him for no less an offense than insincerity. After citing one or two unconvincing examples of Yeats' artificial or "quaint" diction, Orwell wearies of the job, leaving it for some more thorough Marxist. His failure to prove the case does not alter his conviction that it could and should be proved—as though pretentious diction and insincerity were crimes against democracy.[11]

It is clear in this essay and in others Orwell wrote that "literary fascism" is easier to intuit than to establish by textual analysis. It is also clear that Orwell is troubled by a double standard which even he is obliged to resort to in judging artists. That he and Yeats (a genius capable of moving him) should be on opposite sides when the barricades were raised, and that Wodehouse (whom he outgrew in boyhood) should be his ineffectual ally! Perhaps it only confused the issue to know how a poet voted in elections or how he treated his housekeeper. Perhaps, also, it was not safe to let anyone push the world in the direction he wanted it to go—to propagandize under cover of fiction or, as a commissar of public morality, to decree which yogis were politically safe.

Nevertheless, the persuasive power of the written word, the urgency even of fictional prose, was a power Orwell could not help wanting to enlist in the struggle against the oppressors of mankind. There was a subtle kind of propaganda in good fiction and poetry just as there was in good bad fiction and poetry. In essay after critical essay Orwell attempted to define the extent of an artist's responsibility not to his craft but to the human race as a whole, that is, his political responsibility.

Had Orwell declared that instead of being propaganda, all art is moral, he would have raised fewer eyebrows, and had he postulated that every act today is a moral act—including trivial acts that were once decently obscured from public view—he would have made his political point. As it is, he said something even clearer philosophically and practically about writers in a world dedicated to its own destruction: "you can only create if you can *care.*" [12] Caring about art for its own sake was not enough with the world in a state that threatened creative artists even more directly than it threatened progress toward economic goals. In his essay on Charles Dickens Orwell concedes that it is "not necessarily the business of a novelist, or a satirist, to make constructive suggestions." But in any fiction worth taking seriously there is an implicit view of the world which is essentially moral; and a "merely moral criticism of society," Orwell suggests, may be "just as 'revolutionary' . . . as the politico-economic criticism which is fashionable at this moment." [13]

Orwell's criticism surely reflects less the "politico-economic" bent of his socialism than his moral preoccupations. He was distinctly uncomfortable, he confesses, with a writer like D. H. Lawrence who sympathized "about equally" with good and bad characters.[14] He was much more comfortable with

Dickens, whom he commends for siding with the underdog. Quite apart from his literary merits, Dickens was right as a human being. He was generously aroused by injustice, and his "bourgeois mentality," although it contrived no panacea for the world, took for granted the redeeming power of common decency. Orwell calls Dickens a "nineteenth-century liberal, a free intelligence, a type hated with equal hatred by all the smelly little orthodoxies which are now contending for our souls." [15]

In "Raffles and Miss Blandish" Orwell remembers with fondness a "gentleman" burglar, one Raffles, fictitious product of a time "when people had standards, though they happened to be foolish standards." In the English manner of Raffles, would-be gentleman, what is done or what is not done is as irrational, Orwell admits, as a primitive taboo but has the same binding force: "everyone accepts it." He experiences a sharp sense of moral dislocation when, in contrast to Raffles (who was out to make a haul solely to secure his shaky social status) he comes across the characters of a more recent English "who done it," *No Orchids for Miss Blandish*. They are motivated uniformly to pursue power, in variously violent forms, for the sake of power. As though this pursuit were not senseless enough in itself, Orwell perceives that the distinction between the law-abiders and the law-breakers no longer separates the good guys from the bad. He had naively supposed that if "one must worship a bully, it is better that he should be a policeman than a gangster" [16] and that the problem of "how to prevent power from being abused"—a problem admittedly unsolved [17]—should be decided on the side of law and order, that is, common assent and social stability, rather than on the supposition that might makes right.

Though he had "no particular love for the idealized 'worker,'" Orwell did not have to debate which side to take when he was confronted with "an actual flesh-and-blood worker in conflict with his natural enemy, the policeman." [18] Something there was that did not love a cop. Even so, he did not make the typical British mistake (which he describes in *Down and Out in Paris and London*) of confusing the unwashed with the criminal, or the bobby of a corrupt but parliamentary government with the personal storm troopers of leaders who ruled by decree. For those born weak or those rendered helpless by circumstances there had to be legalized protection from the powerful. What alarms Orwell in the American crime story upon which *No Orchids* is patterned is the disappearance of any distinction between those who enforce and those who break the law. Both worship power, right or wrong. The worship of power and successful cruelty are natural concomitants, as he sees them, of the rise of totalitarianism. The modern crime story is a "distilled version of the modern political scene" in which "mass bombing of civilians, the use of hostages, torture to obtain confessions, secret prisons, execution without trial, floggings with rubber truncheons, drownings in cesspools, systematic falsification of records and statistics, treachery, bribery and quislingism are normal and morally neutral, even admirable when they are done in a large and bold way." [19]

Several years later, when the American craze for violence without scruple had further outmoded purposeful criminality, Orwell deplores the decline of the English murder as he deplored its fictional counterpart in *No Orchids* and sighs, almost nostalgically, for the excitement of the old days when a murder was really a murder and not an accident caused by catatonic agents.

> Perhaps it is significant that the most talked-of English murder of recent years should have been committed by an American and an English girl who had become partly Americanized. But it is difficult to believe that this case will be so long remembered as the old domestic poisoning dramas, product of a stable society where the all-prevailing hypocrisy did at least ensure that crimes as serious as murder should have strong emotions behind them.[20]

By the year Orwell wrote this, 1946, the court of the world had on its docket crimes for which it could devise no commensurable penalties—crimes against humanity they were called, for want of a better way of indicating their enormity. Well before this, Orwell had asserted that modern man believes there is no law: "there is only power." [21] It is fitting that in *1984* nothing should be illegal, since there are "no longer any laws."

Although Orwell did not make it explicit, implicit in the body of his writing is a distinction between "orthodoxy" and "ideology" on the one hand and, on the other, "standards" (both of taste and of conduct) and "law." A self-proclaimed socialist, he was not a predictable partisan and, if given the choice between anarchy and orthodoxy in politics or morals, quite likely would have chosen anarchy. It was better to be in doubt than to see doubt vanish from human affairs. But he did not like anarchy—a state in which nothing is illegal. A world where anything goes seemed as reprehensible to him as a world where everything is curtailed. It troubled him that there were no laws to govern the artist except the undefined internal laws that were alleged to govern the particular created world of a painting or a novel. He attacked violence and immorality in the subject matter of art as energetically as he attacked them in the world of men and governments without distinguishing one as a conceptual or symbolic construction of pigment or words and the other as the place where men inescapably lived and suffered. He was concerned that the artist be morally, if not politically, correct and only late in his life disabused himself of this notion and consigned it "to the nursery" along with the "lingering belief that every choice, even every political choice, is between good and evil, and that if a thing is necessary it is also right." [22]

"Benefit of Clergy: Some Notes on Salvador Dali" is particularly symptomatic of Orwell's unwillingness to separate artistic excellence from subject matter and from the ethical tenor of the artist's life. He attacks Dali not for any political penchant but for a "direct, unmistakable assault on sanity and decency," on "life itself"—for crimes against humanity, so to speak. That Dali, in faction-torn Spain, played both ends against the middle and, during World War II, cared about nothing but eating well was enough to alert Orwell to his political irresponsibility; but Orwell relates the egoism of the man to the failure of the artist. He puts the man on trial in order to condemn the artist, much as the Americans (whom Orwell contemns for it) jailed Al Capone for income-tax evasion because they could not apprehend him for murder. Orwell grants that Dali has "exceptional gifts" and an exceptional capacity for hard work. But Dali's autobiography "stinks" in his fairly fastidious nostrils. It reveals what Orwell expects: that Dali is unworthy of his exceptional gifts—in fact, an "undesirable" in the human community. Should Dali's stature as an artist entitle him to benefit of clergy? Not if, as an artist, he works hard to a harmful end.

But, as Dali's accuser, Orwell finds himself in company he dislikes and devotes a considerable part of his critique to baiting the "high-brow baiters." He disassociates himself from their crude tactic of impugning what they can't understand. But if Scylla lies there, Charybdis lies to the other side, and he disassociates himself as vehemently from the art-for-art's-sakers, who were, in his view, "high-brows." Orwell names his own dilemma in steering a course between these alternatives—both of which seem to him humbug. "Obscenity is a very difficult question to discuss honestly. People are too frightened either of seeming to be shocked or of seeming not to be shocked, to be able to define the relationship between art and morals." [23] Again he tasks the Marxist critics for failing in the essential work of critical definition. They are quick enough to smell what "stinks" and to label it bourgeois degeneracy, but name-calling, Orwell complains, is not enough. One should be able to say, "at least in imagination," that a book or picture is good, *and* that "it ought to be burned by the public hangman."

In trying to turn what one *should* be able to do into what one *can* do, Orwell draws an untenable analogy between artists who encourage "necrophilic reveries" and common criminals, maintaining the first do more harm than the latter. Yet he concludes that he would not, after all, burn Dali's pictures, because they "probably cast useful light on the decay of capitalist civilisation." Dali's diseased intelligence then becomes Exhibit I in Orwell's case against the "world's illness." Private vices become public virtues.[24]

Here Orwell is in no better case than the brother who assures Browning's Fra Lippo Lippi that his painting "serves its purpose": in a kind of two-minutes hate, the "pious people" vent their rage upon the painting which depicts the villainous slaves who turn the "Deacon's spit." So Orwell permits Dali's art to stand as an object lesson in necrophilic preoccupations.

One feels, however, that Orwell is enraged with Dali because he disobeyed Fra Lippo's private injunction: to paint the "beauty and the wonder and the power,/ Changes, surprises" in the world and "count it crime/ To let a truth slip." For that, art is given, so that those with exceptional gifts can lend their vision to the ungifted. Dali obviously did not care for the spiritual or political health of the world. Orwell obviously did. Why, then, if the world was fatally sick—perhaps even "dead and rotting"—did Orwell himself write novels which did not "necessarily" have any power to cure or to resurrect? Why did he devote so much attention to the non-political writing of his contemporaries and predecessors? Why, even if his devotion to literary matters was not as exclusive as James' or Joyce's, was he a man of letters and not a man of public affairs?

There is no dissembling in Orwell's urging a relationship between art and politics. What he cared about was a world politically safe not only for democracy but for the autonomy of the artist; and the world in which the artist worked and to which he bequeathed the enduring products of his work was menaced as never before in history, menaced by a new breed of men who were pre-eminently the enemies of mankind. When Orwell could not fight them with a sword, he fought them with a pen. His starting point, he declares in "Why I Write," was "always a feeling of partisanship, a sense of injustice. When I sit down to write a book, I do not say to myself, 'I am going to produce a work of art.' I write it because there is some lie that I want to expose, some fact to which I want to draw attention, and my initial concern is to get a hearing." [25] In so far as Orwell was a partisan, he took the part of the true against the false, the sincere against the insincere, the weak against the strong, the life-lovers against the death-wishers, the artist against the hangman.

Even Orwell's "esthetic enthusiasm" is a partisan concern. As long as he lived, he promises in "Why I Write," he would "feel strongly about prose style." "Good prose is like a window pane," he writes, and orthodoxy "of whatever color" in its demand for a "lifeless, imitative style" is its arch-enemy.[26] Orwell's insistence upon clarity is bound up not only with his "esthetic enthusiasm" but with his "historical impulse" to make a true account of things for posterity and with his moral concern that the truth be reverenced for its own sake. In "Politics and the English Language" he holds insincerity responsible for the deterioration of English, whether that insincerity is unconscious—that is, merely *thoughtless,* as it is likely to be in an age of ready-made phrases that predetermine content—or deliberate, as with those who have motives for obfuscation. The hardening of language into cliché, the abuse of language in verbiage, abbreviation, ugly synthetic locutions, and the cynical perversion of language to say *"the thing which is not"* horrified Orwell esthetically and ethically. He grieved to see the variety, subtlety, and nuance of English lost, just as he grieved to see the dreariness of public architecture and the depersonalization of private housing.

But a loss of flexibility and variety meant also a loss of precision and expressiveness, a constriction of the range of concepts one could articulate, a loss feelingly described in the appendix of *1984,* which examines the political *raison d'être* of Newspeak: the prevention of "thoughtcrime." The concern of official etymologists (there is no other kind in 1984) is to make literally unthinkable any heretical thought by ridding language not only of ideologically offensive concepts ("badthink") but of vocabulary in excess of the most rudimentary utilitarian exchanges. Since much human talk is non-utilitarian, this destruction of words makes incommunicable and eventually inconceivable a number of previously cherished and significant experiences. In political oratory ("largely the defense of the indefensible") "duckspeak" is perfected: the brain idles while appropriate political noises issue from the larynx.[27] The purpose of language is thus perverted, the symbols devised solely for the urgency of expressing meaning are rendered void of meaning, and the "reduced state of consciousness" necessary to perfect orthodoxy is assured. "Orthodoxy," as Syme explains in *1984,* "means not thinking—not needing to think." Huxley's brave new world achieves much the same result with soma; but the outstanding feature of Orwell's superstate is a monumental inefficiency, the purpose of which is to ensure the futility of all human endeavor and, in effect, to rob existence of its organic semblance: growth, becoming. "Nothing is efficient in Oceania except the Thought Police."[28]

An "esthetic enthusiasm" for language is a care to keep it alive, that is, responsive to man's expressive needs. The death of language in prospect, its noticeable atrophy in present use, agitated and dismayed Orwell both as a private man with an emotive life demanding expression and as a political animal, capable of reason and unwilling to be deprived of his distinctive birthright: the tools of logical thought and the means of preserving an accurate record of his life and times.

As a recorder of his life and times, Orwell was often bold in making judgments but painstaking in setting forth what his experience and intelligence found to be "true facts." He kept a tight rein on his "historical impulse" and, noticeably in *Homage to Catalonia,* resisted the temptation to pose as an authority on events he had a part in making. The Spanish conflict, after all, was an incredibly complex business, which had left few, if any, reliable records officially or journalistically and which he had observed at best partially and, he assures his reader, partisanly. The armchair liberals at home irked him as much as the Nationalist and Communist propagandists, both because they did not act upon their professed convictions and because they accepted, wholesale, ideological distortions of a significant historical struggle. With these self-styled internationalists who during the thirties were content to "snigger at every English institution from horse-racing to suet puddings . . . chipping away at English morale . . . sometimes violently pro-Russian, but always anti-British," he was ruthless: "England is perhaps the only great country whose intellectuals are ashamed of their own nationality," he declares and predicts that, if England is to withstand the power-worship prevalent on the continent, patriotism and intelligence will "have to come together again."[29] From Orwell's point of view, in trying to remain ideologically in fashion, the "countless English intellectuals who kiss the arse of Stalin" were no different from "the minority who give their allegiance to Hitler or Mussolini."[30] Granting that "official war-propaganda, with its disgusting hypocrisy and self-righteousness, always tends to make thinking people sympathise with the enemy,"[31] Orwell emphasizes that the "irresponsible carping" of these intellectuals was possible only because they were not and did not expect to be in positions of power.[32]

Orwell's disdain for intellectuals on the Left who espoused "smelly little orthodoxies" is as intense as his dread of fascists on the Right. The disaffection of "thinking people" from their country's cause became ludicrous and dangerous if they merely exchanged patriotic humbug for the official war-propaganda of the enemy. It was bad enough that mass emotion, directed by "newspaper and radio hypnosis," could be "turned on and off like a tap"; no one really expected the masses to be much more acute politically than Boxer the horse, whose mottos in *Animal Farm* make for blind obedience to his leader.[33] But the expedient pacifists who switched mottos overnight with no "intervening stage" of reasoning and no "sense of incongruity," who shouted one day "War is hell" and the next day "War is glorious" merely because the "political landscape" had changed, qualified as experts in doublethink (suppressing the truth one has espoused and then forgetting that one has suppressed it), or—as it is called in *Animal Farm*—blackwhite.[34] The humorless, robot-like aspect of party-liners during the thirties surely provided Orwell with the prototypes of Party members in *1984* and the principles of Newspeak. What Orwell witnessed in his time was the degeneration of political writing into propaganda, which consisted "almost entirely of prefabricated phrases bolted together like the pieces of a child's Meccano set. It is the unavoidable result of self-censorship. To write in plain, vigorous language one has to think fearlessly, and if one thinks fearlessly one cannot be politically orthodox." [35]

During the Spanish Civil War, what shocked Orwell was not really the Fascist version of the struggle, which was, of necessity, pure fantasy; what shocked him more than all the lies of military expedience was the Communist propaganda which could have no effect but to reduce military morale and discourage co-operation among the Loyalist factions. The war, he came to realize, was "above all things a political war" in which the Communist Party, by opposing the workers' revolution for an egalitarian society, was in effect at the extreme right.[36] He learned that those who support totalitarianism, however speciously leftist, all "dread the prospect of a world of free and equal human beings." [37] The brief foretaste of democratic socialism Orwell had in Catalonia in 1936 was, he knew, too good to last. For a few months hope had been "more normal than apathy or cynicism"; the word *comradeship* had "stood for comradeship and not, as in most countries, for humbug. One had breathed the air of equality." The air was inevitably polluted by the systematic lies of political opportunism which, in the name of the workers, betrayed their revolution and set out to convince innocents abroad that freedom is slavery. The genuine camaraderie of equals fighting for their liberty against oppressors of whatever party, like the jubilant struggle of the animals against their masters in *Animal Farm,* was no more than a "temporary and local phase in an enormous game . . . being played over the whole surface of the earth." [38]

The most telling effect of the Communist propaganda (the ludicrous libel of Anarchists as "fascists" in Franco's pay, for example) was to make "serious discussion impossible" among the Loyalist groups and to bamboozle fellow travelers abroad —and among these were not the workers but the intellectuals who, with no outward sign of perplexity or sense of disaffection, did a rightabout-face as often and as mindlessly as drill troups. In Spain Orwell learned that "the clue to the behaviour of the Communist Party in any country is the military relation of that country, actual or potential, towards the U.S.S.R." [39] Potentially, a democratic socialism in Spain was a greater threat to the U.S.S.R. than a monarchist regime or personal dictatorship; hence the need to malign those factions which were not animated or controlled by the Party line. In the strategy of ideological warfare it was impossible for any writer or journalist "fully sympathetic to the U.S.S.R." to do anything but "acquiesce in deliberate falsification on important issues." [40] To Communist propagandists the success of the Loyalist forces was secondary to the issue of political orthodoxy.

Certainly Orwell's experience in Spain complicated the good and the bad of the issues that had impelled him to go there, but it did not make him cynical. Looking back on the Spanish War, he could conclude that there is "hardly such a thing as a war in which it makes no difference who wins." [41] It was somehow better to have fought and lost than never to have fought at all. "To survive you often have to fight, and to fight you have to dirty yourself. War is evil, and it is often the lesser evil. Those who take the sword perish by the sword, and those who don't . . . perish by smelly diseases." [42]

In *1984* Winston Smith also believes some kinds of failure are better than other kinds: "I prefer a positive to a negative." Fighting losing battles has always carried with it a poignant heroism. As long as a failure goes on record, it remains a significant gesture. The experience in Spain worried and saddened Orwell not because his side lost but because, as he remarked to Arthur Koestler, who understood just what he meant, "History stopped in 1936." In Spain Orwell saw "history being written not in terms of what happened but of what ought to have happened according to various 'party lines.'" He feared "that the very concept of objective truth" was disappearing and that nothing could prevent official lies from passing into the record. Granting that history has never been free of errors and distortion, Orwell protested what he found "peculiar to our own age": the "abandonment of the idea that history *could* be truthfully written." [43] The "friends of totalitarianism" in his own country, Orwell charged, postulated that "since absolute truth is not attainable, a big lie is no worse than a little lie. It is pointed out that *all* historical records are biased and inaccurate, or, on the other hand, that modern physics has proved that what seems to us the real world is an illusion, so that to believe in the evidence of one's senses is simply vulgar philistinism." [44]

The concept that right and wrong, true and false, were as relativistic and indeterminable as time and space seemed to Orwell to destroy the assumption men, however opposed to each other, had always been able to make: that there was at least a body of "neutral fact" upon which they could agree. In some way such agreement testified to their common humanity, to their being "all one species." The denial of an objective truth upon which men can agree takes away their *common* sense of the world in which they have acted and makes for a "nightmare world in which the Leader, or some ruling clique, controls not only the future but the *past*"—can decree, in effect, that two plus two equal five.[45] By 1943 at the latest, Orwell had the germinal idea for *1984*. In 1946 he asserted:

> The organized lying practiced by totalitarian states is not, as is sometimes claimed, a temporary expedient of the same nature as military deception. It is something integral to totalitarianism, something that would still continue even if concentration camps and secret police forces had ceased to be necessary. . . . From the totalitarian point of view history is something to be created rather than learned.[46]

Since this "created" nightmare world robs life of even its vestigial meaningfulness in the twentieth century, Orwell, like Winston Smith, "even from the point of view of survival" realized it was better "to fight and be conquered than to surrender without fighting." [47]

One smelly disease Orwell was determined not to perish by was the anemic orthodoxy that afflicted the "left-wing parties in the highly industrialized countries"—a kind of *petit mal* to which professional humanitarians in general were prone. Perhaps because Orwell was politically and emotionally close enough to them to risk contagion, he knew how easy it was—full of good food and good wine—to tell lies in prose, to duckspeak propositions the validity of which had never been put to the test. He excoriated the left-wing intellectuals not only for their egregious distortions of history but for their hypocrisy, for sniping at the very imperialism, for example, which through economic exploitation made their civilized lives possible and their Marxism a "sham." They enjoyed freedom from political responsibility because someone else was doing the dirty work for them.

In his defense of Rudyard Kipling as a spokesman for British imperialism, Orwell discerns that those who rule are obliged to confront practical realities and decide not upon theoretic panaceas but upon *what to do*—an obligation government oppositions are *not* under. Stiff-necked and unimaginative as imperialist policy might have been, Orwell observes, it made one simple, unquestioned assumption, which was moral as well as political: the leaders who assumed responsibility had to bear it, however distasteful the acts consequent upon that responsibility might be. Kipling, like the imperialism with which he was allied in spirit, had this "sense of responsibility" to an eminent degree.

From his early role as subdivisional police officer in Burma, Orwell knew how fatal sensibility and imagination could be in one who ruled. Called upon to deal with an elephant which endangered the community and all too sensible of the conflicting pressures upon him, Orwell learned that to be responsible was to act, and to act was to be damned, whatever he did. The dilemma posed itself in purely emotional terms at the time: he was paralyzed between "hatred of the empire" he served and his "rage against the evil-spirited little beasts who tried to make [his] job impossible." [48] Because of the uniform he wore and because of the mob of natives at his back waiting for him to inflict upon a possibly manageable animal the death that his rifle symbolized, he was driven to the expedient of acting like a sahib, however irrational or unjust such a course might prove. He had forfeited his right to be a spectator to someone else's mistakes. He had lost his freedom from political responsibility, and later in his life, when occasion arose, he could admire the honest if limited, sincere if unexamined assumptions that underlay Kipling's fictional world. The sahib was understandably the butt of ridicule and criticism among circles of refinement and discernment at home, but Kipling at least saw "clearly that men can only be highly civilised while other men, inevitably less civilised, are there to guard and feed them." [49] Orwell had an abiding contempt for men who bit the hand that fed and sympathized with the enemies of those that guarded them.

Even before the English socialists had shown their colors in the Spanish struggle and the second world war Orwell sensed what their ideology meant to them. In *Keep The Aspidistra Flying* Ravelston's girlfriend, secure in her money and modernism, assures the worried editor: "Of course I know you're a Socialist. So am I. I mean we're all Socialists nowadays. . . . You can be a Socialist *and* have a good time, that's what I say." [50] And in the same novel Gordon Comstock, whose political sympathies are as ambiguous as his social status, is suspicious of ideologies that get implemented. "There's only one objection to Socialism," he taunts Ravelston, "and that is that nobody wants it." What *would* Socialism mean in practice?

> Oh! Some kind of Aldous Huxley *Brave New World;* only not so amusing. Four hours a day in a model factory, tightening up bolt number 6003. Rations served out in grease-proof paper at the communal kitchen. Community-hikes from Marx Hostel to Lenin Hostel and back. Free abortion-clinics on all the corners.[51]

Socialism, like the Catholic Church and suicide, Comstock says, is simply a "standing temptation to the intelligentsia." The first world war, the monstrous industrial and political developments after it, the unspeakable meaninglessness of life in England, were enough, George Bowling declares in *Coming Up For Air,* to start anyone thinking, if not to make a

Bolshie out of him. In fact, "every intelligent boy of sixteen is a Socialist. At that age one does not see the hook sticking out of the rather stodgy bait." [52] If between the two major wars of the twentieth century no socialist program appeared on the political scene in England, it was because "no one genuinely wanted any major change" and revolutionary politics was largely a "game of make-believe." [53]

The left-wing intellectuals—paradoxically those who gave evidence in writing of wanting to push the world in a particular direction—come again under Orwell's bitter attack in his essay on Henry Miller, "Inside the Whale." Here Orwell examines, almost as though against his will, the alternatives for a writer in an age when all issues seem political, "and politics itself is a mass of lies, evasions, folly, hatred, and schizophrenia." [54] The year is 1940, and the state of the world is perilous if not intolerable for the writing of novels: the "age of totalitarian dictatorships—an age in which freedom of thought will be at first a deadly sin and later on a meaningless abstraction"—will destory the writer's world. "For *as a writer* he is a liberal, and what is happening is the destruction of liberalism." The novel (a "Protestant form of art"), because it is a "product of the free mind, of the autonomous individual," can be written only by "people who are *not frightened*." It will not be written, therefore, by the "orthodoxy sniffers, nor by people who are conscience-stricken about their own orthodoxy." [55]

But the question with Miller is not even one of orthodoxy. Because Miller is completely apolitical, he seems to Orwell to acquiesce in the state of the world. And yet *Tropic of Cancer* Orwell pronounces a "remarkable book" and pauses to consider the incongruity of his reaction.

> When *Tropic of Cancer* was published the Italians were marching into Abyssinia and Hitler's concentration-camps were already bulging. . . . It did not seem to be a moment at which a novel of outstanding value was likely to be written about American dead-beats cadging drinks in the Latin Quarter.[56]

In the same decade other writers busied themselves hammering Marxism "into a new shape" every time Stalin "swapped partners." Their political commitment was that of men uprooted from a traditional orthodoxy: God was dead, but Stalin, thank god, lived; and, having experienced nothing but "liberalism" in their own country, Orwell charges, they swallowed the stodgy bait of Marxism. Unlike these "orthodoxy sniffers" so afraid to offend the political air over Moscow, Miller remained unperturbed by noises to the left or the right. He chose, says Orwell, to dwell inside the whale, in the veritable womb of Leviathan. He made, in effect, a "declaration of irresponsibility" and preserved a quietism just "short of being dead." [57]

Although, Orwell concedes, "a novelist is not obliged to write directly about contemporary history," he who "simply disregards the major public events of the moment is generally either a footler or a plain idiot." [58] Since *Tropic of Cancer* has convinced him that its author is neither, Orwell proposes two explanations for Miller's quietism: "either complete unbelief or else a degree of belief amounting to mysticism." For a creative writer, he reasons, "possession of the 'truth' is less important than emotional sincerity." An "untrue belief" in literature may be more "sincerely held than a 'true' one." Novels, he concludes, present merely the "truth about the individual reaction." [59]

Miller's voice, to Orwell's ears, is that of the "ordinary, non-political, non-moral, passive man," the "human voice." He supposes that like the common man Miller is passive by political choice, content to keep his own house in order but as helpless against historical forces as against the elements.[60]

T. S. Eliot, whose political and religious principles Orwell surely considered the result of an "untrue belief," nevertheless receives in this essay on Miller the most exalted of Orwell's critical encomiums. As a creative writer during the troubled teens and twenties of the century, "by simply standing aloof and keeping touch with pre-war emotions," Eliot did more to carry on the "human heritage" than those "committed" writers of the thirties who played *Simon Says* with Stalin. Orwell recognizes finally the necessity for a writer to be, above all, with no "sermons," true to the "subjective truth." And on the basis of this subjective truth, Orwell conjectures incredulously, "apparently, it is still possible for a good novel to be written." As though a good novel were ever written on any other basis!

But despite this affirmation of the artistic as distinct from the journalistic or historic truth, Orwell pronounces what he considers Miller's withdrawal as a *politically* significant act, a willful retreat from the only *seemingly* different "swindles" of progress and reaction, a defeatism which robs reality of its terrors by simply submitting to them.

> Get inside the whale. . . . Give yourself over to the world-process, stop fighting against it or pretending that you control it; simply accept it, endure it, record it. That seems to be the formula that any sensitive novelist is now likely to adopt.[61]

Orwell's reluctance to accept this formula makes the word *sensitive* almost pejorative. The novelist who abjures his political responsibility to stand and be counted—or shot down—can't 'take it.' He is good for nothing, by implication, *except* writing novels. Like the cat in *Animal Farm,* he votes on both sides of the issue, or if he does not equivocate, simply escapes, he is like Mollie, who prefers blue ribbons and sugar lumps to "volunteer" labor for the common good.

Orwell's ambivalence toward the writer's role in these essays is obvious. He defends Dickens, Kipling, Wodehouse, Miller and T. S. Eliot apparently because he sees something in them that he cares about—that deserves championing against charges of social irresponsibility. His role of devil's advocate eventually, of course, drove him to consider more and more directly the case he was pleading. In "Politics vs. Literature" he asks to what extent one's enjoyment of a particular work of art depends upon one's agreement with its author's opinions. Although he is unwilling to admit that literary excellence is a thing fully separable from its subject matter, he concedes that a certain "intellectual detachment" enables one to "disagree" with a writer and yet perceive his merits. Enjoyment, however, is another question: sheer literary talent cannot persuade one to enjoy, he says, a book which is "truly wounding or shocking." For purposes of argument, he grants that there may be "such a thing as good or bad art." And, if there is, then the excellence or lack of it must inhere "in the work of art itself." If a book seems "really pernicious" and "likely to influence other people in some undesirable way," Orwell suggests skeptically, one simply devises esthetic standards to disprove its literary merits. "And yet," he admits, upon occasion, "enjoyment can overwhelm disapproval, even though one clearly recognizes that one is enjoying something inimical."

Orwell's instance to prove the possibility is his own perennial enjoyment of *Gulliver's Travels.* He does not for a moment deny Swift's literary ability (although even here he puts *good* in disclaiming quotation marks) but refuses to attribute his "enjoyment" solely to that. Wounding and shocking as *Gulliver's Travels* is, he decides, and diseased as Swift's world view is, one feels the partial truth Swift enunciates: "the part which he abstracts from the whole does exist," however one shrinks from recognizing it.

Can a book, then, be "good" if it expresses "a palpably false view of life"? The "best books of any one age," Orwell observes,

> have always been written from several different viewpoints, some of them palpably more false than others. In so far as a writer is a propagandist, the most one can ask of him is that he shall genuinely believe in what he is saying, and that it shall not be something blazingly silly. . . . The views . . . must be compatible with sanity, in the medical sense, and with the power of continuous thought: beyond that what we ask of him is talent, which is probably another name for conviction.[62]

In *Gulliver's Travels,* because of the intensity of Swift's conviction, a "world view which only just passes the test of sanity is sufficient to produce a great work of art."

Orwell's ambivalence toward "great works of art" the world view of which he disapproved might have been dispelled had Orwell admitted the distinction between the discrete disciplines of art and history, or art and ethics for that matter. His failure to distinguish the separate areas of human experience these disciplines are bound to be true to is the unimportant failure of a writer who would have scorned the role of esthetician and never presumed to be a philosopher. Neither, for all his protests, was he a propagandist. What moved him to write —essay or novel—was what he cared about. He knew which truth he was after instinctively, if not theoretically, and his apparent guilt about writing merely novels may have sprung from his sense that novels were true only to the "subjective reaction," a reaction which, without verification from one's fellow men, might be a form of insanity. Relentless, Orwell pursued the elusive truth of historical fact, returned in exposition to what was verifiable by document and eye-witness. The created realities of the novel must have seemed sham to him. After all, unlike the "facts" of history, they held still. They were always the same. They were eternal. And today they alone assure Orwell's immortality—a difficult enough achievement in a world encroached upon by anonymity, meaninglessness and death.

However misdirected in particulars, the intensity of conviction in Orwell's own world view produced in his critical writing a discernment of artistic sincerity and in his fiction a subjective sense of the world imperiled by malign forces. He cared and, without a boundless fund of inventive ingenuity, he created, achieving the final luminosity of *Animal Farm* and the political novel *par excellence, 1984:* a tragedy of personal heroism in a mechanical "world-process" which mangles the individual as purposelessly and cruelly as ever the ancient fates kept Oedipus alive in order to teach him he was dead.

In some way that had nothing to do with subject matter, however, Orwell sensed that a novelist, by virtue of what he produced ("the product of rationalism, of the Protestant centuries, of the autonomous individual"),[63] was in the simple practice of his craft *"against* totalitarianism" as much as any democratic socialist. And what the artist bequeathed to the world strengthened the world by proclaiming the human essence. In much the symbolic way the coral embedded in crystal subtly threatens the Party in *1984* and incriminates him who owns it, imagination and a love of truth in writers (even a love of prose style) destined them to be the inveterate heretics of ideologies and orthodoxies. Explicitly political or not, they would be suspect under a totalitarian system.

The relation between art and politics, if we judge by the two rich essays he devoted to the subject in the late forties, tantalized Orwell to his dying day. In "The Prevention of Literature" he reaffirms his belief that "[a]bove a quite low level, literature is an attempt to influence the viewpoint of one's contemporaries by recording experience." Freedom of expression, he argues, concerns the "most 'unpolitical' imaginative writer" as vitally as the expositor. Censorship of the news, proscriptive and prescriptive regulations of journalistic freedom, had become controversial even in democratic countries obliged to weigh the whole truth and nothing but the truth against the expedients of national security and partisan loyalties. Not only the journalist but his readers were conscious of the "unfreedom" in news media which threatened, in addition to the professional integrity of these media, in the long run any reliable historical accounting of events.

But Orwell's main interest in "The Prevention of Literature" (1946) and "Writers and Leviathan" (1948) is the plight of the creative artist, who is "unfree" in a less spectacular way if he is compelled "to falsify his subjective feelings" —the "facts" which constitute his subject matter.

> He may distort and caricature reality in order to make his meaning clearer, but he cannot misrepresent the scenery of his own mind; he cannot say with any conviction that he likes what he dislikes, or believes what he disbelieves. If he is forced to do so . . . his creative faculties dry up.[64]

Can the "imaginative writer" get inside the whale—merely observe, record and remain noncommittal? Not in an age in which all issues are political issues. Under repressive conditions one's private feelings may be the most controversial subject of all. There is, Orwell reasserts, "no such thing as genuinely non-political literature"; "fears, hatreds, and loyalties" are inextricable from the modern political atmosphere. "Even a single taboo can have an all-round crippling effect upon the mind, because there is always the danger that any thought which is freely followed up may lead to the forbidden thought." [65] It is one thing for a politician to switch his loyalties; his activity is inevitably bound into a network of compromise and expedience. But a writer who is forced to switch his loyalties must "tell lies about his subjective feelings, or suppress them altogether. In either case he has destroyed his dynamo. Not only will ideas refuse to come to him, but the very words he uses will seem to stiffen under his touch." [66]

Sincerity, again, is Orwell's touchstone for the creative writer. He foresaw that even a Yeats or a Dali, compelled to rejoice in a workers' paradise of equality, sobriety, and propriety, might suffer an atrophy of creative gifts which would render those gifts nugatory. The imagination, Orwell concludes, "like certain wild animals, will not breed in captivity." [67]

It is significant that Orwell, against his egalitarian instinct and his aversion to benefit of clergy, here devises a special category for the artist and distinguishes the creative writer even from the journalist as a species which can thrive only under the most inviolable autonomy. One should be able, in theory at least, to demand that the artist comply with prevailing standards of morality and decency and objective standards of social and political truth. But more precious than such public government of conduct and belief was the thing that ruled private feeling with an absolute tyranny of its own: total honesty or nothing. The artist was different from his fellow men. For most people the problem of personal integrity and public allegiance, Orwell writes, does not even arise:

> . . . their lives are split already. They are truly alive only in their leisure hours, and there is no emotional connection

> between their work and their political activities. Nor are they generally asked, in the name of political loyalty, to debase themselves as workers. The artist, and especially the writer, is asked just that—in fact, it is the only thing that politicians ever ask of him. . . . But his writings, in so far as they have any value, will always be the product of the saner self that stands aside, records the things that are done and admits their necessity, but refuses to be deceived as to their true nature.[68]

The artist, then, whatever civic role he plays (in war or in elections, for instance) must keep "inviolate" the self which makes his work possible.

Orwell in these two essays also entertains the possibility that in an "age of faith" there might exist no disruptive conflict between the artist and the prevailing orthodoxy. Perhaps, he concedes, an orthodoxy which had been long enough established to be taken indifferently would leave "large areas" of a writer's mind unhampered by his official beliefs. Totalitarianism, however, Orwell fears, promises not so much "an age of faith as an age of schizophrenia," in which neither the stability of objective truths nor the "emotional sincerity . . . literature demands" can be tolerated. The prevailing orthodoxy would be *totalitarian,* that is, totally proscriptive and prescriptive not only of subject matter and attitudes but of the language in which they might be couched. For all its purposes, book-writing machines, fed on formulas and prefabricated phrases, would do a more reliable job than writers; and, since tyranny is one of the themes that "cannot be celebrated in words," the writer would have to choose between "silence and death." [69]

Believing that, even in countries dominated by no official ideologies, political responsibility had become synonymous with "yielding oneself over to orthodoxies and 'party lines,' with all the timidity and dishonesty that implies," Orwell confronts the paradox that his own critical and personal creed as a writer made inevitable; and he declares unequivocally that "acceptance of *any* political discipline" is "incompatible with literary integrity." A writer's political and religious beliefs—even if they are as seemingly apolitical as pacifism and personalism—are "poisonous to literature. . . . Indeed, the mere sound of words ending in -ism seems to bring with it the smell of propaganda. . . . As soon as they are allowed to have any influence, even a negative one, on creative writing, the result is not only falsification, but often the actual drying-up of the inventive faculties."

Here Orwell makes it clear that all art is *not* propaganda, that the two are, in fact, irreconcilable: "To yield subjectively, not merely to a party machine, but even to a group ideology, is to destroy yourself as a writer." What, then, is the answer? To abjure politics? Emphatically not: "To lock yourself up in the ivory tower is impossible and undesirable" in an age like ours. Orwell pleads simply for a "sharper distinction" between political and literary loyalties and suggests a kind of bifurcation of functions for the writer as creator and as political animal. Political responsibility has little to do with ultimate truth, and political action is of necessity expedient—a means to an end, a doing of "certain distasteful but necessary things" without the concomitant "obligation to swallow the beliefs that usually go with them." What is necessary is not necessarily "right." Political decisions propose ugly alternatives, and one is forced to choose "which of two evils is the less." One can resolve the dilemma frequently only "by acting like a devil or a lunatic."

> When a writer engages in politics he should do so as a citizen, as a human being, but not *as a writer.* I do not think he has the right, merely on the score of his sensibilities, to shirk the ordinary dirty work of politics. . . . But whatever else he does in the service of his party, he should never write for it.[70]

In effect, what Orwell demands of the writer is no less than "most people" have already accommodated themselves to: political assent, even co-operation, in the means to necessary ends, and at the same time rejection of the ideology which envisions these ends. On the one hand, the writer must fearlessly pursue thoughts he knows to be heretical and scorn the risk of being condemned. On the other hand, when his "writings and his political activities . . . actually contradict one another" and when such contradiction seems "plainly undesirable," Orwell does not suggest that the writer abstain from political action—certainly not that he "falsify [his] impulses." The remedy, Orwell says, is "to remain silent."

Orwell impales himself on both horns of the dilemma here. Because politics is a mass of lies and a choice of evils, because right and wrong are forever relative in the sphere of action, all honest men, not just writers, it would seem, must be schizophrenic, and the difference among them dependent solely on whether they consciously suffer the discrepancy between their impulses and their actions or, without admitting the discrepancy, slip painlessly into lunacy. The paradox comes up again and again in Orwell's writing and is perhaps its single most powerful generative idea. Committed himself to the goal of the left orthodoxy—"a viable form of society which large numbers of people actually want"—he realized that his fellow travelers toward this goal could not admit their ideological "falsities" nor discuss openly the problems that give rise to them. Modern men, Orwell maintains, are all to some extent victims of "perfectionist philosophy" and become obscurantist when actuality belies their beliefs. "Hence there has arisen a sort of schizophrenic manner of thinking, in which words like 'democracy' can bear two irreconcilable meanings, and such things as concentration camps and mass deportations can be right and wrong simultaneously." An orthodoxy always contains "unresolved paradoxes." One can reason from empirical data to valid conclusions only "if one is privately disloyal to the official ideology." [71]

We will probably never know on how many or how serious occasions Orwell himself, noting the discrepancy between his private conclusions and official ideology, remained "silent." But one is persuaded by the number of times he attacked the orthodox and insisted upon seeing the discrepancy between the private truth and the public lie that he seldom followed his own "remedy." For to have remained "silent" would have been to do away with his inviolate self as effectually as a public hangman might; and one doubts that, after all Orwell had to say about the pernicious effects of self-censorship, he acquiesced in this schizophrenic tyranny beyond concessions to tactfulness in direct confrontation or patriotism in England's dark hours.

There is certainly little evidence in Orwell's critical essays that the partisan feeling out of which he said he wrote distorted the evidence he examined. At most, that feeling abstracted and gave shape to the moral questions that arise from the total import of an artist's work. In Orwell's fiction, partisan causes invariably yield to the created life of his characters, who may have come into being originally as denouncers of imperialism, capitalist exploitation, or commercial depredations, but who in the end obey "private feelings" that have nothing to do with official beliefs.

If in his fiction and criticism Orwell fused "political purpose and artistic purpose," it was because he cared about the human essence and feared its enemies. In the mundane drama he conceived, the "great death wish of the modern world" is personified as a gigantic robot of man's invention, foot poised to smash the face of the sleeping protagonist. What would rouse the sleeper? The sound of exploding bombs? The duckspeak of political oratory?

The silent, ageless mirror held up to life—which never so much as clouded with the sleeper's breath—might have no power to alarm or to make constructive suggestions, but by keeping touch with men's emotions it carried on the "human heritage." The artists preserved the subjective truth of being. The historians preserved the notable deeds and words of men for the "use of posterity." The polemicists pushed the world in the direction they wanted it to go. But before any of these could operate people had to be kept alive, and this specifically political task occasionally curtailed or forfeited the freedom of artists, historians and polemicists alike.

For there were those who created because they cared and those who destroyed because they hated. Much as he dreaded the hardening of heartfelt truths into official dogma, Orwell had the political sense to know that history abhors a vacuum and that the commissars would rush in where yogis feared to tread. Precisely because it was a necessary evil, because it took precedence over what outranked it in the scale of values, the political sphere required the utmost vigilance, lest the guardians of public safety and morality became the inquisitors of private conscience and delivered into the hands of the hangman not only the criminal but those who slept inside the whale.

In a democracy, Orwell could admit no freedom from political responsibility, even for the artist, but he did come to see that art was a means to a political end only because its truth was a recording of subjective feeling—from the merest visceral twinge to the magnificent, barely sane obsessions of mystical insight—and such truth was "*against* totalitarianism." The artist's work, however, was a "thing apart" from politics, and his autonomy as a worker had to be guaranteed by political means; for he, of all the workers of the world, was as a worker the most easily debased.

CHAPTER TWO

A BELLY WITH A FEW OBSOLETE ORGANS

. . . the belly comes before the soul,
not in the scale of values but in point of time!

—Orwell, "Looking Back on the Spanish War," in "Such, Such Were the Joys"

Before thought was replaced by orthodoxy and action by movements, it was not only the rich who had time to be bored. Properly speaking, the rich suffered ennui—a more exquisite affliction than Orwell permitted himself. The boredom which he knew well and which promised such hollow horrors on a large scale comes from idleness which cannot be construed as leisure. The rich, after all, "can afford to be intelligent" if they choose, but the "first effect of poverty is that it kills thought." Orwell's devout student of the subject, Gordon Comstock, learns that it is "in the brain and the soul that lack of money damages you." [1]

World weariness itself becomes a bore to a healthy man, and Orwell so loved the world that when he was wounded in Spain his immediate reaction was a "violent resentment" at having to leave a place which, everything considered, suited him so well: "I thought what a good thing it was to be alive in a world where silver poplars grow." [2] Three years before his death he reaffirmed his love for "the surface of the earth" and his endless pleasure "in solid objects and scraps of useless information." [3] The natural beauty of the planet which is man's home was in no more danger of palling on him than the inexhaustible complexity of the world man made upon the planet to outlast himself and commemorate his activities. "It's easy enough to die if the things you care about are going to survive," George Bowling declares in *Coming Up for Air.*[4] Whether you die or stay alive doesn't matter, Winston Smith echoes in *1984,* so long as human beings stay human.

But sometimes it is difficult to stay human, even if you are survived by what you care about. Those who *don't* care don't count. The hysterical dilemma of the jaded rich—"What shall we do tomorrow/ What shall we ever do?"—concerned Orwell less than a vision of the brown shades passing over London Bridge, the hollow men, the empty men, circling the prickly pear, the lonely men in shirt sleeves surveying from their rented rooms the soot from chimney pots, the refuse heaps in vacant lots, and debris of neglected alleyways. Like T. S. Eliot, Orwell was moved by such images to the perception of "some infinitely gentle/ Infinitely suffering thing" in the landscape of modern industrialism. When a man's environs from birth to death were slag heaps, he could not even by dint of imagination believe that silver poplars survived, somewhere, untarnished by soot.[5]

Before the shadow fell between the idea and the reality, Orwell made his move—from theoretic Socialism to the life of those it was designed to rescue. *Down and Out in Paris and London* is a record of his descent to the underworld.

There he discovered that poverty is not "complicated" or "terrible" in itself; it is "merely squalid and boring." The "enforced idleness" of a man without money in Paris or of a vagrant in England, along with the uselessness of his sufferings, is the most demoralizing effect of poverty Orwell lists. Boredom and futility—whether he encountered them in the dull, lifeless jargon of political oratory or on a London street corner idling until he could redeem his meal ticket—affected Orwell so adversely that he could imagine no unhealthier climate than one in which they prevailed as the rule rather than the exception. Boredom and futility plagued the troops with whom he fought on the Aragon front, and it is not hard for him to suppose that the English were reading *No Orchids for Miss Blandish* to escape "the boredom of being bombed" —exceeded only by the boredom of waiting to be bombed.

In *Down and Out* Orwell attacks the prevailing popular image of the tramp as a filthy, vaguely sinister character, antisocial in his refusal to be productive. He found few "impudent social parasites" among the men with whom he consorted: a tramp was "only an Englishman out of work, forced by law to live as a vagabond." The simple expedient of enabling the unemployed to stay in one place and develop a self-sustaining community through their own labor never occurred to official imagination, which worked on the assumption that the only way to keep tramps out of trouble was to keep them on the move. In consequence, Orwell found himself conscripted into an army of—for the most part—able-bodied men forced by the vagrancy laws to march "up and down England like so many Wandering Jews." The circuit they described from one "spike" to another was a treadmill to nowhere which it was impossible to get off despite good intentions and sanguine expectations of returning to normal life. The vagrant, Orwell concluded, "lives a fantastically disagreeable life, and lives it to no purpose whatever." [6]

Undertaken in the name of efficiency in dealing with a social problem, the regimentation of these grey hordes resulted in a waste of human resources that appalled Orwell, whose conscience was as frugal as any northman's conscience and as offended by poor husbandry. Unless a man were an impudent parasite, Orwell learned, he preferred the most taxing, demeaning labor to having nothing to do and no role but that of ne'er-do-well. The sheer futility of thousands of men milling about their native land from one dirty bed to the next may have suggested to Orwell the dreadful potential behind the idea of regimentation: men could be permanently engaged in meaningless motion for the political purpose of denaturing them as human beings. The ideologies of the twentieth century are embodied as parties and become known, curiously, as movements; but their goal is the ultimate stabilization of erratic individual directions. They move in ever-narrowing circles toward an absolute zero at which molecular activity—and with it what characterizes life—ceases.

Now English officialdom, Orwell knew, was not in the grips of a political ideology but under the influence of a false moral preconception: the English are a "conscience-ridden race," and poverty is closely associated in their minds with sinfulness. At havens for vagrants run by the Salvation Army, the "detestable evil" of gambling, along with the commensurate evils of smoking and talking, was proscribed very much as though it were responsible for the condition in which a vagrant found himself. All conscience-ridden Anglo-Saxons know the devil makes work for idle hands; the unemployed are consequently in the devil's employ. By singing a few penitential hymns (the equivalent to Orwell of having to give assent to the proposition that two and two equal five), a man could take a bath—for cleanliness is next to godliness—and fill his shrunken belly with bread and margarine. In return for this charity, he was obliged to show not that he was a self-respecting fellow but that he knew his place as a supplicant. He had to comport himself, while in the Army's barracks, with an appropriate blend of piety and "abject, worm-like gratitude" and agree to have his pleasures dictated by his benefactors. The Salvation Army refuges may well be the prototype for the state-operated grog shop which, in *1984*, dispenses gin to the imbeciles released by the Ministry of Love and other assorted undesirables.

The evils of futility and boredom, of course, are aggravated by a host of other discomforts, the most grievous of which is perpetual hunger: "every tramp is rotted by malnutrition"; a "man who has gone even a week on bread and margarine is not a man any longer, only a belly with a few accessory organs."[7] The food he gets is unpalatable and unsatisfying, like the food served in *1984* to Party members in ministerial cafeterias. Poverty furthermore cuts a man off from "the whole race of women." Moneyless, as Gordon Comstock discovers, a man is "unlovable." No woman will let him beget his children. He "feels himself degraded to the rank of a cripple or a lunatic." His alternatives are to become a pervert or to turn celibate.[8] Denied effectually, if not officially, the chance to beget his children, he is potent to no purpose, powerless to ensure even his biological continuance. In all respects he is an "undesirable" excluded from the rolls of the living. The recipients of General Booth's charity might well pray—as Comstock prays—"Give me not righteousness, O Lord, give me money, only money." [9]

In Paris Orwell found the quality of poverty somewhat different. There the life of a menial was onerous and degrading because he labored under conditions which worked in every way against his accomplishing simple, routine tasks. A job in the kitchen of a swank Paris hotel was not so much boring as it was frenzied, frustrating, and exhausting. Again Orwell is shocked at the waste of man-power, shocked that in the most civilized capital of the technologically advanced western world chaos, filth, and primitive facilities persisted. French inefficiency, like the English inefficiency of maintaining able-bodied men on the dole, was not the result of official malevolence, though it was conceivably the result of subtle snobbery operating within luxury establishments: the difficulty of performing one's duties was in inverse proportion to one's status. But Orwell postulates an attitude toward labor which unofficially holds that drudgery is a good in itself for the lower orders, "for slaves, at least." The attitude is not the punitive one of the conscience-ridden English but rather "fear of the mob." The entrenched interests, Orwell argues, have little to fear from a mob of menials who lack the leisure or the energy to devise changes.[10] And so the inefficiency continues, and, however much pride the menial takes in overcoming obstacles by exertion and ingenuity, his efforts are fundamentally "useless" in being grossly out of proportion to what they need be.

(Orwell is less convincing when he argues the uselessness of luxury as such. The rich who frequent the luxury hotels in which menials slave under medieval conditions would be more comfortable and eat more sanitary meals if they stayed at home. Why should they spend exorbitant sums to eat badly? O reason not the need!)

Poverty in Paris, however, Orwell reports, was not totally villainous. For all its power to degrade and to vitiate human effectiveness, it formed a rich compost of organic life in which certain desirable traits of the human race thrive. The street scene Orwell paints of a "representative Paris slum" is alive with color, odor, motion, and sound; it is a sketch for the district in *1984* where the "proles" are loosely confined: "a dirty place, but homelike," as Orwell describes his quarters in Paris, with "good sorts" and "eccentric people" whom poverty had freed from "ordinary standards of behavior." [11] The bistro is a "cheery" spot, and the indefinable camaraderie, recaptured there night after night, by implication is an invincible enemy of totalitarian efficiency, regimentation, and "rightthink." The "proles"—always the last group in any civilization to be enfranchised—have one inalienable right: the right not to think. The "great redeeming feature" of down-and-out poverty is that it "annihilates the future" and divests the present of disturbing significance.[12] A *plongeur,* Orwell learned from direct experience, cannot afford a sense of honor. "How right the lower classes are!" Comstock muses enviously before he himself hits bottom.[13]

The "lower classes," historically bond-slaves of one ruling group after another, are first of all numerically important to the vision of democratic socialism. In the twentieth century, for the first time, their liberation is not an impracticable dream but a material possibility. From his self-imposed deprivation Orwell knew what Conrad's Marlow knows as he contemplates the future of young Jim: "it is not the haunted soul but the hungry body that makes an outcast. . . ." [14] To Orwell the frightening fact about those excluded from a significant role in human commonwealths (as about the millions of political prisoners who disappeared forever behind barbed wire in the twentieth century) is their anonymity. They leave behind them no record of the life they have lived —except the massed effort of their organic body implicit in monuments attributed to their rulers.[15] In *1984* they are both the hope and the despair of Winston Smith. They alone are "free" because, like animals, they are beneath suspicion of thought. Because they lack "general ideas," their discontent can lead nowhere. When Smith buttonholes the ancient prole to verify his suspicion that life has not always been as it is under the Party, he discovers that the memory of this oldtimer is "nothing but a rubbish heap." He is a drivelling, unenviable *"Struldbrugg."* [16]

The mindlessness of the masses is the unavoidable consequence of the labor by which they support the civilized concerns and the refined indulgence of the few. Their entire energy is expended to fill the belly of mankind, and the stupefying purchase of this expenditure is, ironically, not discontent but a kind of contentment, the kind that Boxer, the indefatigable "worker" of *Animal Farm,* enjoys. Exhausting labor of any kind at least keeps a man from ennui and from paying any heed to his precious sensibilities and his varicose veins. Before he meets Julia, the greatest pleasure Winston Smith has is his "work"; and, whether she is absorbed over the fumes of the glue pot or teaching runny-nosed ineducables [17] or picking hops in a state of amnesia, Dorothy the clergyman's daughter knows the joy of "a life that wore you out, used up every ounce of your energy, and kept you profoundly, unquestionably happy." After a day in the fields she is stupid with "an almost beastlike heaviness." [18]

The trouble with the life of the field worker is its sleeplessness and exposure:

> To live continuously in the open air [as beasts live], never going under a roof for more than an hour or two, blurs your perceptions like a strong light glaring in your eyes or a noise drumming in your ears [devices used in 1984 to dull perceptions]. You act and plan and suffer . . . as though everything were a little out of focus, a little unreal. The world, inner and outer, grows dimmer till it reaches almost the vagueness of a dream.[19]

Such a life, then, entails the loss of precisely what distinguishes human from plant and animal life: consciousness of the processes taken to keep alive and intelligent determination of the reasons for taking the trouble. Field workers are, in more than a geographic sense, transients. Like menial labor of any kind, their labor leaves no mark on the record of human achievements and resembles the drudgery which engages the Ministry of Truth whenever Oceania swaps partners. Every "historical" detail of the years during which she has been at war with the "wrong" enemy must be "rectified"—that is, falsified—a perfectly stupendous labor, a "mighty deed" which, by its very nature, can "never be mentioned." [20] It is a deed which will be performed, with ever-increasing difficulty, as often as realliance demands, and it signifies precisely nothing, except that there is no past and no present or future different from the past—only the meaningless substitution of one piece of nonsense for another, motion within a movement toward oblivion. Even those then who have been liberated from the proletariat are enthralled in a timeless trance that has the "vagueness of a dream."

In *1984,* the greater the demands of a job upon a man's intelligence and ingenuity, the farther removed his accomplishment from what is necessary to sustain life and to render it significant. A Party worker is in effect a ward of the state maintained at minimal operating capacity for the sole purpose of *destroying* significance, whether he fabricates history, mass-produces "art," "creates" human nature closer to the Party's desire, or rids language of its emotional import. He is robbed of any satisfaction work can yield except the "beast-like heaviness" of total exhaustion. He is a belly with a few specialized organs.

In addition, like the down-and-out of England, the Party member is fed unwholesome, nauseous food; he is conditioned to regard sexual pleasure as unattainable; and he is least at home where he rests his head—and his vigilance. The proles alone enjoy that dangerous and desirable thing called "own-life"—and, tragically, the fact has no political consequence. Their freedom from thought makes them in effect "orthodox" —that is, unconscious—and their freedom from political responsibility ensures nothing but their perpetual enslavement. The cheery bistros of the prole district are simply places where the Circe of cheap booze can convert what remains of their manhood into swinishness.

Significantly, the only pub frequented with impunity by a Party member (and then only when his uselessness has been assured) is the Chestnut Tree Café, the official hangout for derelicts who have betrayed the last citadel of humanity, the heart. There, from time to time, a "cracked and jeering note, a yellow note," comes from the telescreen—"only a memory taking on the semblance of sound" to intensify the misery of those whose lives have the blurred outlines of a dream. A tavern chair is no longer what Sam Johnson called it, the "throne of human felicity." And the café is no longer a spot where lovers tryst, where friends hold intense, intimate, carefree exchanges, where a man can be at his solitude and yet not lonely, the presence of his fellowman and the world's unceasing commerce assuring his leisure, no longer a clean well-lighted place away from his rented room and curious conscience. Such a place has become "only an 'opeless fancy" which "passed like an Ipril dye" long before Winston Smith reached drinking age.

The work-horses of the world, Orwell knew, unless they united in conscious purpose, would like Boxer eventually be sent to the "knacker's"—a metaphor which has frightening force since the advent of human rendering plants. As things stood even in the technologically advanced mid-century, life's unalterable law for the masses, as Benjamin says in *Animal Farm,* still decreed "hunger, hardship, and disappointment" with no reasonable expectation of radical change for the better or for the worse. But Boxer is at least memorialized by a few of the lower animals who remember with love his selfless dedication to solidifying the gains of the revolution they made in common. In *1984,* however, drudgery is denied even this remote solace. Parsons, a Party worker of "paralyzing stupidity" and "imbecile emotions" whose sweat is an occupational affliction, is done in by his own offspring. By that time it is "normal for people over thirty to be frightened of their own children."[21] As long as party workers deferred religiously to their leaders and saw the solution to every problem simply as "I will work harder," Orwell knew it would take no more than a child to betray them.

Family solidarity, the "ownlife" that could still be enjoyed by autonomous units in a hostile world, was a bulwark against such betrayal. During World War II Orwell expressed fear that "private liberty" in England was a "lost cause": an 'opeless fancy ruthlessly sacrificed to the expedient of survival. His pessimism was tempered, however, by the conviction that this lost cause was worth fighting for, since the alternative was not worth surviving for. And it still seemed to him, as it seems to Bowling in the late thirties, that although the "prole suffers physically" he is "a free man when he isn't working." [22] Orwell could not let himself believe that the life of the English masses, however unconscious, was inconsequential. For one thing, there was the English habit of clinging obstinately "to everything that is out of date and a nuisance" (as "ownlife" increasingly seems to streamlined modern systems). Even the vagrants clung to the delusion that they would, tomorrow, step off the treadmill and become self-respecting subjects of His Majesty. In fact, Orwell relied precisely upon the uncritical power of the English to take action "without taking thought," to draw instinctively together during crises, regardless of class, and to be guided by an unquestioned code of conduct, never formulated but universally understood. Miraculously, the British had hung on to the outmoded belief in individual liberty, however they allowed their leaders to circumscribe it in emergencies: the liberty "to have a home of your own, to do what you like in your spare time, to choose your own amusements instead of having them chosen for you from above." [23] The "privateness of English life," however, was not a national resource shared by the really down-and-out. A man who did not have even beastly work to do became, in fairly short time, less than a man, a creature unable to fill his own belly—let alone the belly of a family—and yet unable to think beyond the present needs of his belly. As long as a man struggled to stay in the ranks of the respectable, he could be counted in the census. Orwell carefully distinguishes down-and-out poverty from genteel poverty. The first demanded an abdication of "ordinary standards of behavior." The second demanded an excruciatingly hard effort to preserve them, to keep up appearances, to escape having one's poverty detected. Upon this effort, Orwell believed, the entire ingenuity of England's lower middle class was spent. He admired the pluck this effort took while he only grudgingly admired the ruse of gentility maintained by the impoverished: that one did *not,* like a wild animal, live *only* to eke out subsistence in the midst of economic perils. The clergyman's daughter, for example, is hounded by the demon of respectability and unpaid tradesmen. The unwritten commandment of her society is the one Gordon Comstock formulates: "money is virtue and poverty is crime." [24] Respectable poverty is the most oppressive kind, Orwell insists. If it continues any length of time it exhausts the very resourcefulness it requires. The rationale of those clinging to the under side of the lower middle class is: this is not the worst, so long as we can say this is the worst—an old English sentiment from a tragic context. Comstock, brewing tea in his room to save a few pence and disposing of the tea leaves furtively in the w. c., is as good a figure of this genteel struggle as any.

Gordon Comstock's trouble is that he is *not* just a "walking stomach." His brain and soul already damaged by lack of money, he torments himself by imagining the miserable lives concealed by the façades of dingy buildings. The "sense of disintegration" endemic to his time is strong in him as he considers how many cigarettes he has to last him till pay day. In the advertising posters across the street he reads "prophecies of doom," behind the hearty commercial grin, "nothing but a frightful emptiness, a secret despair," in fact, the "great death-wish of the modern world." [25]

Comstock revolts against a civilization which worships Mammon and against the big lie this meretricious deity exacts from its devotees. Just as the more hyperbolic the "advert" the worse the product, so the more "respectable" a man's job the more it degrades his integrity. Like Winston Smith, Comstock tries to create a world independent of the world he hates, something durable and significant "*outside* the money-world." His effort is a pretentious satiric poem, fortunately for the world never completed, which he calls "London Pleasures."

But you can only create if you can care; and, until he ceases to care about anything, Comstock cares about nothing but divorcing himself altogether from the world as he finds it. His pen failing his revolutionary purpose, his descent toward the oblivion of destitution is suicidal. His own great death-wish lures him away from not only commercial dishonesty but whatever makes life meaningful. He does not escape life, however, "merely by taking refuge in dirt and misery. . . . Going to the devil isn't so easy as it sounds. Sometimes your salvation haunts you down like the Hound of Heaven." [26]

In the drab mechanized world of the twentieth century, the indigent have but two salvations short of the Salvation Army: work and love. Comstock disdains the world's work and, impoverished and joyless, cannot get on with the work he wants to do. "Invention, energy, wit, style, charm—they've all got to be paid for in hard cash." [27] Furthermore, as one of the predictable consequences of his willful poverty, he has suffered sexual deprivation. "How damned unfair it is that we are filled to the brim with these tormenting desires and then forbidden to satisfy them! . . . It seems so natural, so necessary, so much a part of the inalienable right of a human being." [28]

And so it is, as long as human beings stay human. But, down-and-out, Comstock is less than human. Poverty crushes even desire out of him finally. His appetite dies as his stomach shrinks. His salvation arrives in the form of Rosemary, who, for all her unquestioned lower-middle-class morality, out of the magnanimity not of sexual desire but of *caring* for Comstock, gives herself to him when he is good for absolutely nothing but the will-less begetting of a new life. He marries Rosemary, in his turn, not out of middle-class scruples, but for the same reason the poor have always married. "If marriage is bad," as Comstock acidly admits, "the alternative is worse." [29] Or, as Doctor Johnson says, "Marriage has many pains, but celibacy has no pleasures." The poor man thinks: " 'I cannot be worse, and so I'll e'en take Peggy.' "

Comstock is unexpectedly relieved and pleased to resume the burden of his own life and of two additional ones. "To abjure money is to abjure life," he concludes,[30] and a rather cynical conclusion it sounds if one dwells simply on the indignity of his writing commercials in abject defeat at the altar of the money-god. The point is, though, that while the world demands he prostitute his talent as a writer, he carries with him now a world of his own to which he can escape. When the baby quickens in Rosemary's womb, a "strange, almost terrible feeling, a sort of warm convulsion," stirs in its father's entrails: "For a moment he felt as though he were sexually joined to her, but joined in some subtle way that he had never imagined." In a way that cannot be imagined until it is experienced, man and wife is one flesh; their union multiplies their separate powers and increases life. Comstock kneels, almost reverently, his head pressed against Rosemary's body, listening.

> He could hear nothing, only the blood drumming in his own ear. But she could not have been mistaken. Somewhere in there, in the safe, warm, cushioned darkness, it was alive and stirring.[31]

However obscure to the world, in this safe darkness lies proof that Comstock also is "alive." Since he is potent, the money-god is not omnipotent after all. The failure of Comstock's conscious revolt serves as a kind of chastisement to a hero who determines to be poor when he doesn't have to be. As Doctor Johnson also says, "When I was running about this town a very poor fellow, I was a great arguer for the advantages of poverty; but I was, at the same time, very sorry to be poor."

Now Orwell was a great arguer for doing away with poverty, at the same time that he was very sorry to subscribe to the cure. His instinct warned him that the patent medicines might be worse than the "scathful harm" itself. It was true that under the laissez faire of British economy a man, like Comstock, opposed to the prevailing philosophy that "money is virtue," suffered if he took his own way against the way of the world. It was true also that the genteel, whom nothing short of total amnesia could cause to forget "ordinary standards of behavior," were as flotsam at the mercy of tidal forces once their credit or their meagre competence ran out. But, although Comstock willfully and Dorothy haplessly endure the worst effects of both genteel and down-and-out poverty, it is only in Orwell's last two novels that poverty becomes a tangible political issue. In *Animal Farm* and *1984* the onerousness of labor and the unpleasantness of existence are not incidental to particular unfortunates or "casuals." They are instituted as a rule of life for everyone except the rulers.

The animals of Manor Farm revolt because their discontent happens to get formulated simply enough for them to understand: they want shorter hours, more to eat, and a guarantee that they can retire in peace and security. Under the "collective oligarchism" which replaces capitalistic exploitation, however, even well-disposed outsiders observe that the lower animals do more work and receive "less food than any animals in the country," and suffer without respite until they drop from exhaustion. All their property, to be sure, is "public" now, but it is administered by the revolutionary leaders (their new masters) to insure economic inequality. As Emmanuel Goldstein explains in *1984*, "the only secure basis for oligarchy is collectivism. Wealth and privilege are most easily defended when they are possessed jointly." [32]

On the farm, as in Oceania, the "general state of scarcity increases the importance of small privileges and thus magnifies the distinction between one group and another." Everyone is equal, but some are more equal than others—a truth which the pigs, contemptuous of the mentality of the lower animals, declare publicly but which Winston Smith discovers only when he walks into the luxury apartment of O'Brien and is served wine by a butler. In theory,

> if leisure and security were enjoyed by all alike, the great mass of human beings who are normally stupefied by poverty would become literate and would learn to think for themselves; and when once they had done this, they would sooner or later realize that the privileged minority had no function, and they would sweep it away.[33]

In practice, there was a remote chance—worth taking, in Orwell's estimate—that they might; but there was no guarantee that a new group of oppressors from their own ranks would not rush in to fill the vacuum left by the old.

It might, furthermore, be "later" rather than "sooner" before the great mass of human beings discovered that the broom they owned collectively for sweeping purposes was ineffectual against modern artillery. Orwell trusted the masses to be politically vigilant about as tentatively as he would have walked a rope bridge over Niagara Falls. But one thing he did trust: that, in the long run, "a hierarchical society was only possible on a basis of poverty and ignorance." [34]

This was one of the dangers to which the sleeping masses had to be alerted. In so far as art can be propaganda, *Animal Farm* was Orwell's attempt to push people away from the direction in which he feared unscrupulous leaders might take them. But in so far as Orwell was a Socialist, he was committed to the belief that raising the "standard of living of the whole world to that of Britain would not be a greater undertaking" than World War II had been. He did not claim, however, that "that would solve anything in itself. It is merely that privation and brute labour have to be abolished before the real problems of humanity can be tackled." [35] The belly came first merely "in point of time," and filling it was, in Orwell's opinion, a fundamental humanitarian problem which, in England at least, only the Socialists espoused politically.

It was a problem, though, which Orwell saw might be altogether too easily solved, creating a problem of commensurable dimensions in its turn: a huge vacuum of idleness where the empty belly had been. Paradoxically, the only barrier in this direction was the passive resistance, or the massive indifference, of the British "proles" to revolutionary programs devised as their salvation. Despite the unsatisfying quality of work available to them in modern times, despite the penurious, tedious complexion of their struggle to keep the aspidistra flying, the British masses persevered in their deplorable state with the same mute instinct that caused even sympathetic liberals like himself to cling to the evils they knew rather than fly to those of a futuristic utopia. Ironically,

Orwell discovered a legitimate sense in which it was true that "Ignorance Is Strength." The more intelligent a man, the more orthodox he became when he swung to Left or Right; but it was Orwell's experience that the average worker was supremely and protectively *un*orthodox: "I have yet to meet a *working* miner, steel-worker, cotton-weaver, docker, navvy or whatnot who was 'ideologically' sound." [36] In *The Road to Wigan Pier*—with considerable satisfaction, for all his disclaimers—Orwell informs revolutionaries of various hues what their propaganda is up against.

First of all, it is up against an ingrained middle-class mentality in the English worker. Orwell assures readers of the Left Book Club that for better or for worse his *own* notions "of good and evil, of pleasant and unpleasant, of funny and serious, of ugly and beautiful" are essentially—probably ineradicably—"*middle-class* notions." [37] He lectures the Marxists on the one hand for condemning indiscriminately whatever is middle-class; their attacks upon "bourgeois values" as inherently degenerate, Orwell reminds them, drive away potential converts: "If you want to make an enemy of a man, tell him that his ills are incurable." [38] He reproaches the Marxists on the other hand who, like O'Brien, not only diagnose the fatal malady but know the wondrous cure, who foresee the conclusion of all ills in total mechanization and who, with a vulgar hedonism which displeases him, suppose that man's needs are altogether economic, that for all practical and theoretic purposes man is a "walking stomach," a predictable statistical item.

In extolling the labor-saving machine as the savior of the twentieth century, the economic witch-doctors forget, Orwell says, that man has "a hand, an eye and a brain" which the machine renders superfluous. Orwell knew that for most left-wingers the most cogent argument of socialism was the utopian possibility that, through collective ownership of the modern means of production, what had enslaved man for centuries, his bondage to biologic necessity, would wither away as effortlessly as governments. The very possibility terrified Orwell. He insists that many of the most admirable traits "can only function in opposition to some kind of disaster, pain or difficulty" and that "the tendency of mechanical progress is to eliminate disaster, pain and difficulty." [39]

Of course Orwell did not blame the Socialist for industrial progress per se but for extolling it to the exclusion of goals he thought more central to a revolutionary cause. "The process of mechanisation," he feared, had "itself become a machine, a huge glittering vehicle whirling us we are not certain where, but probably towards the padded Wells-world and brain in the bottle." [40] He feared this process, its seeming inevitability, just as he feared the tendency to regard the cyclic nature of history as a preordained process quite beyond man's intelligent control, like a process of nature. While Orwell's realism did not allow him to dream of a return to pastoral simplicity, he did know that, in the past, history—far from being an irreversible process or a metaphysically ordered progress toward beneficial goals—had more than once been willfully checked in or deflected from its apparent course by those who had enough at stake to stop its impetus. He foresaw also the possibility that just as man had stepped into the processes of nature and countermanded physical laws once they were understood, so when it became clear that the end result of mechanization was an increase in consumer goods which would liberate the "lower orders" and enable them to be economic, therefore political, equals with their oppressors, their oppressors could step into the process and arrest progress at a fixed point. They might also—as they already had in the totalitarian states of the twentieth century—halt history once and for all by substituting ideological humbug for "true facts."

In *The Road to Wigan Pier,* the only tenable goals Orwell admits for Socialism are "liberty" and "justice"; the only "real Socialist" is the man who wants fervently "to see tyranny overthrown"—the tyranny, presumably, not only of capitalist exploiters but of ideas and trends. For all his concern with poverty in 1937 when he wrote *The Road to Wigan Pier,* Orwell obviously had economic objectives less in mind than political ones. All issues had become political issues. His rallying cry to the Left is a political ultimatum: socialism or fascism. Liberty and justice for the individual or worship of the state under a rule of latter-day saints, the megalomaniacal saviors of the poor and the ignorant.[41]

Because in the face of Fascism unanimity of political purpose seemed paramount to him, Orwell urges the Socialists to "humanise" their propaganda, to rid it of the doctrinaire, the eccentric, the merely silly, so that it would not repel the simple worker and not appall the thinking men who were needed in the struggle. (He knew that the leaders in any revolution "would tend to be people who could pronounce their aitches.") [42] He concedes that, at the moment, the choice did not have to be made between an "inhuman world" in which man was mechanized out of existence and a human one in which his hands, eyes, and brain were not teleological anachronisms; but in the second part of *The Road to Wigan Pier* he very clearly shows his aversion to any utopian program and especially to the industrial utopia at the heart of the communist dream which would make the world *less* human than it was.

> The truth is that when a human being is not eating, drinking, sleeping, making love, talking, playing games or merely lounging about—and these things will not fill up a lifetime—he needs work and usually looks for it, though he may not call it work. Above the level of a third- or fourth-grade moron, life has got to be lived largely in terms of effort.[43]

And by "effort" Orwell did not mean the soul-killing drudgery which made man no better than a brute, but purposive exertion, a using up of his peculiarly human potential in meaningful accomplishment—if sheer labor, at least labor which demanded the skills of eye, hand and brain as well as the man-power of brawn, the kind of labor Milton's Adam describes to Eve as a human birthright:

> . . . other Creatures all day long
> Rove idle unimploy'd, and less need rest;
> Man hath his daily work of body or mind

> Appointed, which declares his Dignity,
> And the regard of Heav'n on all his ways.
>
> —*Paradise Lost,* IV, 616–20

Yet when Eve, the original 'totalitarian,' assumes that work is the *sole* purpose for which they were created and devises a scheme to get more of it done, Adam reminds her:

> . . . not so strictly hath our Lord impos'd
> Labor, as to debar us when we need
> Refreshment, whether food, or talk between,
> Food of the mind, or this sweet intercourse
> Of looks and smiles, for smiles from Reason flow,
> To brute deni'd, and are of Love the food,
> Love not the lowest end of human life.
> For not to irksome toil, but to delight
> He made us, and delight to Reason join'd.
>
> —*Paradise Lost,* IX, 235–43

In 1946, in some fairly relaxed "Thoughts on the Common Toad," Orwell does not feel particularly "wicked" or "politically reprehensible"—even as men groan in the "shackles" of capitalism—in suggesting that "life is frequently more worth living because of a blackbird's song" or a "yellow elm tree in October." These things keep alive the human essence infinitely more than political pamphlets. The planting of a tree, he proposes in "A Good Word for the Vicar of Bray," is a non-partisan act of expiation for one's social wrongs and a pledge ("at almost no cost") that man was created not only to toil irksomely but to delight in the earth's surface. He reproaches the political bigots who consider it their duty to be discontented themselves and to keep other people from enjoying life as it is, as though it were "our job to multiply our wants and not simply to increase our enjoyment of the things we have already."

> Certainly we ought to be discontented, we ought not simply to find out ways of making the best of a bad job, and yet if we kill all pleasure in the actual process of life, what sort of

> future are we preparing for ourselves? If a man cannot enjoy the return of spring, why should he be happy in a labor-saving Utopia?

By keeping alive one's childhood response to the beauty of the earth, "one makes a peaceful and decent future a little more probable" and "by preaching the doctrine that nothing is to be admired except steel and concrete, one merely makes it a little surer that human beings will have no outlet for their surplus energy except in hatred and leader-worship." The political malcontents, like the religious zealots, would do away with subjective feelings if they could, but spring, Orwell proclaims, is here, "and they can't stop you enjoying it."

> So long as you are not actually ill, hungry, frightened, or immured in a prison or a holiday camp, spring is still spring. The atom bombs are piling up in the factories, the police are prowling through cities, the lies are streaming from the loud-speakers, but the earth is still going round the sun, and neither the dictators nor the bureaucrats, deeply as they disapprove of the process, are able to prevent it.[44]

For Orwell, bread no more assuages the "hunger of the body" than idleness rests it. If man is no more than a belly, he is in effect no more than a machine which has to be stoked, and the purpose of living is merely to spend man-hours to produce fuel for the machine to consume—a tautology of means and ends which quite excludes "delight" and renders the accessory organs of sex, vision and intellect obsolete. Work, not only as a means of filling a man's belly but of declaring his dignity and expressing the equality of men in their human condition, is nevertheless a central tenet of Orwell's socialism. "Nationalization of land, mines, railways, banks and major industries" means to Orwell in effect that "nobody shall live without working."[45] Such a goal at least aspires toward a condition in which the privileged few no longer are idle to breed mischief out of their exquisite ennui and perpetrate class distinctions on arbitrary bases.

But the kind of work which distinguishes man as Lord of Creation at least in his artificial world and which redeems his need to sweat for his bread becomes less and less imaginable in what Hannah Arendt has described as a society of "jobholders." [46] In the *grosse famille* of the twentieth century, whether it is called The Great Society, Ingsoc, or Big Brotherhood, the ostensible goal is to eradicate the "scathful harm" of poverty which has cursed the human race since long before Chaucer. Planning in the ménage of the social family destines every member to produce and to consume on an ever increasing scale, as though life were one immense peristalsis. (Even the academic has been invaded by this mania. Faculty members either produce or lose their jobs and promotions. Their product feeds the hungry press, just as Shelley and Keats now feed the computers; the press adds its digestive juices and spews the finished product out upon the trade or textbook markets—the latter handling particularly perishable commodities. There the product is consumed—tasted or chewed thoroughly—and then, if not digested in a periodical, remaindered. The universities themselves are under pressure to produce—to turn out so many doctors, lawyers and chiefs per year for the use of Society.)

Taken out of man's hands by the instruments of his own invention, this mechanistic process may result in total consumption, a malady which, unlike the old-fashioned disease, ends with a bang, not a whimper. If man no longer cares, he cannot create and may, out of the absolute boredom and futility of his existence, bomb civilization "to hell where it belongs."

Orwell rejected the fictional possibility of atomic holocaust. He conceived instead another way that total power could be used to satisfy the "great death-wish of the modern world." Like T. S. Eliot, he saw that there was the way of the saints and the martyrs and the way of "most of us." "Most of us" are content that the earth goes round the sun. The saints, if they could, would stop it.

CHAPTER THREE

THE WAY OF THE SAINTS AND THE WAY OF MOST OF US

And yet is not mankind itself, pushing on its blind way,
driven by a dream of its greatness and its power upon
the dark paths of excessive cruelty and excessive devotion?
And what is the pursuit of truth, after all?

—Joseph Conrad, "Lord Jim"

The power of the mind or the spirit to control the body is assumed not only by saints and martyrs but by the modern revolutionary. Knowing that all the "habits of Man are evil," the animals of Manor Farm draft their constitution on the basis of Major's last warning: "No animal must ever live in a house, or sleep in a bed, or wear clothes, or drink alcohol, or smoke tobacco, or touch money, or engage in trade." [1] By virtue of having thought of the possibility and having acted on it, the pigs break all these proscriptions with impunity.

The pigs, as a consequence, are the most human of the animals, in a way. They not only systematize, and thus pervert, a dream into an ism; they take advantage of the illiterate who have no written record of what was originally resolved; they fabricate an eternal counter-revolutionary scapegoat for their failures (Snowball, the deathless enemy of Animalism, plays in *Animal Farm* the role Emmanuel Goldstein is assigned in *1984*); they resume business with their enemies because it is expedient; they divert attention from their outrageous exploitation of the lower animals by shifting alliances with shadowy external foes who constitute a common danger; they silence internal criticism with spectacular purges and trials until a time comes "when no one dared speak his mind, when fierce growling dogs roamed everywhere, and when you had to watch your comrades torn to pieces after confessing to shocking crimes." Smug in the conviction that they themselves cannot be overthrown, the pigs betray the revolution and channel the fruits of labor into their private troughs, perpetuating meanwhile an emergency state of privation, like that of a "besieged city" where "the possession of a lump of horseflesh makes the difference between wealth and poverty." [2] The pigs, feasting and brawling drunkenly with their ideological enemy, are indistinguishable, in the end, from man.

There are, however, much less genial self-proclaimed saints than these pigs. The pigs illustrate cogently the Falstaffian nature of ambition: not only to wear clothes but to wear the softest silk, to skim the very cream pots of the earth without so much as milking a cow. The pigs' gluttony and indolence are as notable as the propaganda and storm-troopers by which they terrify the animals and persuade them that material rewards and happiness must be postponed indefinitely. But in *1984* the aim of the Party is not business as usual, a resumption of the eternally infernal human condition, but the end of human affairs altogether, totalitarianly. In *1984* the human essence itself is the proclaimed enemy; and, as Orwell says in his essay on Gandhi:

> The essence of being human is that one does not seek perfection, that one *is* sometimes willing to commit sins for the sake of loyalty, that one does not push asceticism to the point where it makes friendly intercourse impossible, and that one is prepared in the end to be defeated and broken by life, which is the inevitable price of fastening one's love upon other human individuals. No doubt alcohol, tobacco, and so forth, are things that a saint must avoid. . . .

Yet many people "genuinely do not wish to be saints, and it is probable that some who achieve or aspire to sainthood have never felt much temptation to be human beings." The would-be saint's longing for "non-attachment" springs, Orwell says, from "a desire to escape from the pain of living, and above all from love, which, sexual or non-sexual, is hard work." [3]

In *1984* the Party cannot abide imperfection. "It is intolerable to us that an erroneous thought should exist anywhere in the world, however secret and powerless it may be," O'Brien tells Winston Smith. At last human perfectibility is possible. Technological and psychological means detect and narrow the range of remaining error. There are no longer martyrdoms for lost causes.[4] The Russians, the first historically to realize they must bring their enemies over to their side by forced confessions, are now regarded as crude pioneers. The Party has surpassed them: it makes the confessions true. It is not content with the confession of heresies at the stake; it changes the heretics into true believers.[5] The stages by which this is accomplished (in mid-century called "brainwashing") are the stages by which all mystics have been initiated to ultimate truths and been enabled to bask in eternal light.[6]

Man is at the mercy of many things which make sainthood, or even heroism, difficult, and perhaps the greatest of these is his body and its capacity to feel. Hunger, cold, exposure, pain, and innumerable minor irritants and discomforts attend his struggle to survive in war or peace. Orwell frankly admits that in Spain he feared the cold worse than the enemy; and he never forgot that, however malleable one's overt conduct or how changeable one's convictions, "*physical* feeling" remained "fundamental," unassailable and unassimilable to whatever rational codes of behavior one subscribed to. At root, it is "physical repulsion" that turns the bathed and scented intellectual or white-collar worker, however poor he may be, against the laborers with whom he should join: *"the lower classes smell."* [7] It is "physical repulsion" that ruins marriage as a haven for Dorothy in *A Clergyman's Daughter* and makes Flory's birthmark hideous to Elizabeth in *Burmese Days*. And in *1984* Smith is brought to the final stage of acceptance by something so physically repugnant to him that he sacrifices love and what remains of his mind to avoid it. After their separate sojourns in Room 101, Smith and Julia both know that the Party has a way of making you care about nothing but yourself. "And after that, you don't feel the same toward the other person any longer." You are released from the pain of loving.

A Party member knows at best only what he is, not what he may be, for the Party has at last found a use for the "biological uselessness of pain and fear, the treachery of the human body," which "swells up until it fills the universe." [8] There have always been fairly simple ways of making men the slaves of their bodies. The proles are slaves for the simple reason that, although their bodies are still their own, ignorance and inertia keep them from aspiring higher than the most elemental feelings.

Party members, however, because they have the intelligence to conceive of general ideas, are continually harassed by the strident telescreens and kept in a state of low psychic energy by overwork, sexual frustration, bad food and graceless clothes, inadequate heat and plumbing, and a shortage of everything that makes life minimally palatable. If these continual discomforts are not enough to crush humanity out of them, there is always pain, the single goal in 1984 toward which progress has not been halted. Pain is the means the Party has to make its power felt. And of pain, Smith discovers, for all his heroic determination, "you could wish only . . . that it should stop. Nothing in the world was so bad as physical pain. In the face of pain there are no heroes. . . ." [9] Pain ends all loyalties and makes a man incapable of loving anyone but the tormentor who puts a stop to it. Pain and physical revulsion turn him away from the world and break his kinship with its inhabitants. They fill the universe and make conceivable nothing but his inevitable mortality and isolation in the flesh. Individual solipsism, in 1984, is preliminary to and necessary for "collective solipsism." At its crudest, most mindless level, the instinct for survival, something having to do with neither courage nor cowardice, renders survival a living death.

Long before he wrote *1984* Orwell knew that under the stimuli of fear and pain a man's most reasoned loyalties could be countermanded, whether they were commitments to truths or to human beings. When he lived for days under the apprehension of arrest and execution in Spain, he admits, he made none of the "correct political reflections."

> I never do when things are happening. It seems to be always the case when I get mixed up in war or politics—I am conscious of nothing save physical discomfort and a deep desire for this damned nonsense to be over. Afterwards I can see the significance of events, but while they are happening I merely want to be out of them—an ignoble trait, perhaps.[10]

However ignoble, the concern of human beings for their bodily comfort has always kept alive in the race a Falstaffian skepticism about the deeds and policies undertaken in the name of honor, truth, and other Quixotic abstractions. The laugh of the full belly or the mutiny of an empty one is a corrective to those who find quarrels in straws and oblige "little chaps" to dig the pits their bodies will fill. The Sancho Panzas who settle for an occasional joint of roasted meat, a jolly wench, and the sun that dries their dew-drenched clothes are the eternal enemies not only of schemes of perfectibility but even of modest programs of amelioration.

In the same way, the ludicrous and the pathetic, because they remind men they are all the same under the uniforms and party badges, are natural enemies of absolute rule, military or civilian. When Orwell was in the lines on the Aragon front, he and his comrades beheld a Fascist soldier running in full view opposite them, one hand clutching a message, the other holding up his trousers. Why did Orwell not shoot at this rare and excellent target? Partly, he says, "because of that detail about the trousers. I had come here to shoot at 'Fascists'; but a man who is holding up his trousers isn't a 'Fascist,' he is visibly a fellow-creature, similar to yourself, and you don't feel like shooting at him." [11]

From his experience in Burma, Orwell grasped the "futility of the white man's dominion in the East." In turning tyrant he destroyed his own freedom, for the condition of his success as a ruler was that he should "spend his life in trying to impress the 'natives' "—in trying not to seem like a creature who, on certain vital occasions, removed his trousers altogether. For Orwell as an agent of the Holy British Empire not to have confronted the dangerous elephant would have been impossible. The natives would have laughed. "And my whole life, every white man's life in the East, was one long struggle not to be laughed at." [12]

"Whatever is funny," Orwell declares in his essay "The Art of Donald McGill," is "subversive" of the standards society has to uphold for survival. In a free society a balance for which there is no formal recipe is tipsily maintained between Don Quixote and Sancho Panza—between the inherent "hypocrisy" which presupposes an ideal of conduct and the "bawdiness" of sheer animal spirit caught up in the realities of existence. The freer the society, the less dangerous the laughter. The military ballads of the English are as "humorous and mock-defeatist," Orwell says, as English patriotism is unconscious and inarticulate. Military ostentation and braggadoccio are possible only "in countries where the common people dare not laugh at the army"; in England they simply provoke derision. Orwell believed that hatred of war and militarism were "rooted deep" in the English, irrespective of class. The English sword is there, in case it is needed, but because "no Hymn of Hate has ever made any appeal to them," the English work on the unspoken assumption that their sword is best left in its scabbard.[13]

Why did Orwell, who did not shoot the Fascist he had gone to Spain to kill, shoot the ideologically innocent elephant in Burma? Because as a uniformed official he was both superhuman and less than human. In proportion as his power to inspire fear and inflict pain increased, his freedom to act as a moral agent in his own right and to feel as "one of us" diminished; because, as Orwell chose to see it, he was a function of tyranny, and tyranny works only if it does not appear ridiculous to its victims.

The relation of the white man to native populations he rules is analogous to that of adult and child; and Orwell observes that, in the eyes of a child, "an adult who does not seem dangerous nearly always seems ridiculous." [14] It does not occur, for example, to the Malay helmsmen in *Lord Jim* that the white officers could have abandoned the *Patna* because they feared death. White men were no ordinary mortals; they were above fear. They had "secret reasons" for doing what they did, reasons which made them the most inscrutable thing in the whole inscrutable East. So extraordinary is the behavior of Tuan Jim in Patusan that the rumor of his supernatural powers travels as far as Batavia. His feats of strength and heroism are attributed to some secret magic he possesses; and he, who combines in his person the executive, legislative, and judicial powers of rule, is as a father to "his" people.

Jim is, at the same time, nothing but a child, following the shoddy dream of his boyhood imagination up to the last. His dream is none other than carrying the white man's burden with honor, a dream possible only because he never questions the "truth of ideas racially [his] own, in whose name are established the order, the morality of an ethical progress." [15]

Now Jim comes from an English parsonage, from what Marlow calls "that good, stupid kind we like to feel marching right and left of us in life . . . the kind that is not disturbed by the vagaries of intelligence and the perversions of . . . nerves," [16] and even when the dark powers assault him with mindless fear, he never genuinely doubts the "sovereign power enthroned in a fixed standard of conduct." [17] Most Europeans who, flushed with boyish idealism, give their lives to native peoples as Jim does live long enough to discover that they have, in effect, sold their souls to brutes (as Marlow's cynical correspondent puts it).[18] For the natives they govern understand nothing of this "fixed standard" except that *it* mysteriously governs the pale foreigners. The Englishman in the Orient was not merely a figure of tyranny indistinguishable from native tyrants. He was obliged by some unwritten law to behave as he would in England, to preserve an image of himself quite incongruous with his role as imperialist exploiter. Orwell discovered that an Englishman in Burma had to be regarded as a gentleman even if (as Big Brierly says to Marlow about the disgraced Jim) "he ain't fit to be touched." Because some of the Anglo-Indians he knows are no better than Conrad's "Gentleman Brown," Flory in *Burmese Days* is infuriated by the discrepancy between the ideal and the actual; but when the chips are down he sticks with his kind, with the body of men held together in the Orient by nothing but "just the name" for decency and honor.[19]

In *Burmese Days,* the doctor whom Flory befriends, a native as rare in Burma as Dain Waris is in Patusan, is more convinced of the truth of ideas racially *not* his own than any Englishman whose ideas they ostensibly are. Not the validity of the ideas themselves but the hypocrisy or sincerity of the English who espouse them is the subject of endless debate between him and Flory. Ironically, the doctor who believes British idealism to be sincere and adopts a code of conduct not native to him is as close to sainthood as Lord Jim. As an outcast, a member of a lesser breed, he cannot *afford* a lapse from the ideal. Flory, on the other hand, whose role is not simplified by the doctor's willingness to exempt him from even the ethical demands of friendship, discovers that his personal idealism disintegrates with the first brush of reality. Not only has the fixed code of the gentleman no "sovereign power" over him; even his private code of honor—allegiance to his native friends and hostility to the imperialist oppressors—gives way under the stress of mixed emotions.

To be sure, any Englishman less obtuse than Colonel Blimp or Lord Jim suffered in the East an ambivalence of loyalties. Unless he remained a child, he would in time despair of the natives' ever grasping the simplest of his clichés. Surrounded by a crowd of curious "little beasts" waiting to see him shoot an elephant, could Orwell have paused and declaimed upon the sacredness of private property or the economic feasibility of letting the elephant live so that it could do the work of fifty men another day? If not, how could he ever explain that one's word was infallible, that one's burden was moral, that one's laws—the "bloody laws," as Ellis calls them in *Burmese Days,* laws which the rulers upheld even against their strongest instincts—were impartial?

Orwell never saw as clearly as Conrad the subtleties of imperialism, probably because as a democratic socialist he could not admit that what would be good for England might be farcical for his comrades in other countries and could only curse the system which had forced him to find this out. But, like Conrad, he was extremely sensitive to the indwelling spirit of England herself; and it served him, as it serves Marlow, as "a mute friend, judge, and inspirer." To those who return to it from abroad it seems a "disembodied, eternal, and unchangeable spirit" which somehow has a "secular right to our fidelity, to our obedience." [20] Orwell met this spirit when he returned from Spain, and during World War II it made him conceive of those over whom it presided as Marlow conceives of them: "an obscure body of men held together by a community of inglorious toil and by fidelity to a certain standard of conduct." [21] He knew as well as Conrad knew that this mute spirit and the unwritten code had no "sovereign power" over the actions of men. They were not infallible guarantors of "liberty" and "justice." But by their very nature as intangibles they were safer guides to conduct for "most of us" than the absolutes of the saint which denied the flesh and sought through pain to escape the pain of being human.

The indwelling spirit of any land is quite a different thing from a totalitarian "world-view" (as Orwell called it). The spirit of the land is the spirit of its people individually, their fatalism or optimism, their acquiescence or opportunism, in meeting the challenge of life. It is the felt sum of private standards which makes for national unity and underlies that elusive quality called national character.

In defining it, Orwell compares England to a family, a family with "rich relations who have to be kow-towed to and poor relations who are horribly sat upon" and "a deep conspiracy of silence about the source of the family income." Like any family, it is imperfect: the "young are generally thwarted and most of the power is in the hands of irresponsible uncles and bed-ridden aunts. Still, it is a family. It has its private language and its common memories, and at the approach of an enemy it closes its ranks. A family with the wrong members in control—that, perhaps, is as near as one can come to describing England in a phrase." [22]

Upon his return from Spain, Orwell was almost seduced by the quality of life in England: everything was so predictable one couldn't believe things of incredible moment were happening anywhere in the world. To an Englishman who stayed at home, the rights and wrongs were "so beautifully simple." [23] But Orwell had just escaped from the atmosphere which prevailed in Spain after the Communist take-over of government. There, a "vague sense of danger" was perpetual. One felt like a conspirator whatever one did. The "presence of armed men," the changing rumors, the censorship, the arrests without charges or trials, gave one a continual consciousness "of some evil thing . . . impending." [24] The law, far from being impartial, was simply "what the police chose to make it." Decree as the alternative to law and violence as the internal and international alternative to policy had become the rule, Orwell realized, in three European countries other than Spain. Understandably, he was alarmed by the "deep, deep sleep of England" and feared: "we shall never wake till we are jerked out of it by the roar of bombs." [25]

Orwell's impatient shaking of England to no avail is translated into the frustration of his fictitious heroes during the thirties: Flory, Comstock, and Bowling, for all of whom political concerns are really only incidental to private desires. Flory wants companionship in his misery, Comstock wants literary fame, and Bowling would settle for widowerhood. Each has a kind of vindictive desire to see England exploded out of her smugness, her beautifully simple rights and wrongs.

Comstock surveys the squalid lower-middle-class dwellings of the little chaps who don't know or care who pulls the strings that make them dance. Like Orwell, he is half-contemptuous and half-admiring of these job-holders who struggle to keep "respectable" on less money than a navvy gets. Politically and economically they *are* "puppets"; they are "too busy being born, being married, begetting, working, dying" to interest themselves in abstract forces at work on their fate.

> Our civilisation is founded on greed and fear, but in the lives of common men the greed and fear are mysteriously transmuted into something nobler. The lower-middle-class people . . . lived by the money-code, sure enough, and yet they contrived to keep their decency. . . . They had their standards, their inviolable points of honour. They "kept themselves respectable"—kept the aspidistra flying. Besides, they were *alive*. They were bound up in the bundle of life. They begot children, which is what the saints and the soul-savers never by any chance do.[26]

When Comstock chooses the way of the little chaps rather than the way of a saint who worships in sackcloth and ashes an idol of his own devising, he proclaims the aspidistra the "Tree of Life." In the squalid economy of England's working classes, the aspidistra signifies to the world that the householder who puts it in his window behind the lace curtains has just enough affluence to afford something of absolutely no practical—let alone esthetic—value. The damned thing survives not only indifference and neglect but direct physical abuse. Dormant, it husbands its strength to put forth new foliage just when it seems to have died forever. The people whose lives it symbolizes, plant-like, blind, ignorant, grope toward the light, which for Orwell is a simple, unmystical goal: "the decent life . . . now technically achievable." "I myself believe," Orwell wrote in 1943, "perhaps on insufficient grounds, that the common man will win his fight sooner or later. . . ."[27]

The cheap comic post-card was an English staple which intrigued Orwell. It seemed to him to burlesque, to mirror up-side-down, the private system of values which the common man considered universal and more enduring than the actual laws of his country. The laws "are designed to interfere with everybody" and are to be brought into play only—like the British sword—when someone does not know what is cricket. In practice, Orwell observes, the laws "allow everything to happen." This is possible only because, while the common man is not puritanical and the publicans are not saints, the English character is extremely "gentle" and the English attitude toward life "deeply moral." "Public life in England has never been *openly* scandalous," and, unlike the great nations of the Continent, England has never felt obliged to drive "thousands of its nationals into exile or the concentration camp."[28] The Sancho Panza in the common man gives the corrective raspberry to any ideal likely to take over as an ideology. At the same time, when it "comes to a pinch," Sancho can be "heroic."[29]

In his eulogy of 1941, because patriotism on the whole was stronger than either class-hatred or internationalism, Orwell is willing to trust that, in a pinch, the English could be counted on for "swift unanimous action," the kind a family takes in a crisis. He is willing to trust also that, whatever changes in England as a result of the war, the "gentleness, the hypocrisy, the thoughtlessness" of her people will continue to guarantee her stability and continuity with the past: "the reverence for law and the hatred of uniforms will remain, along with the suet puddings and the misty skies"—and, of course, the aspidistras. Even the "hanging judge," no more popular an arbiter in England than the umpire in an American baseball game, will endure as "a symbol of the strange mixture of reality and illusion, democracy and privilege, humbug and decency, the subtle network of compromises, by which the nation keeps itself in its familiar shape"—very much like a living organism which survives by adaptation and the overcoming of obstacles.[30] Patriotism, the cohesive spirit which has so much to do with whether people survive or not, entails, Orwell later wrote, "devotion to a particular place and a particular way of life, which one believes to be the best in the world but has no wish to force upon other people." Patriotism is by nature (unlike what Orwell called nationalism) a purely defensive ism—probably the only one.[31]

"England Your England" was written in a year during which, surely, even whistling in the dark was a modest form of heroism. England politically was on the defensive. However sanguine Orwell appears in this essay, he did not forget how delicately balanced in perilous times—how downright chancey in a world gathering into mass movements under the crusading banners of various ideological truths—such a thing as British constitutionalism was. What, exactly, did the constitution say? Was it written down? Did anyone have a copy of it? Confronted by the great crisis of the twentieth century—the rapid advance of totalitarian systems upon the free areas of the world—were the little chaps any more secure than the farm animals who have never had the leisure to learn reading?

The character who best expresses Orwell's prewar apprehension is George Bowling in *Coming Up for Air* (1939). Like other countries in the western world, England has suffered badly from post-world-war disillusionment and the ensuing period of economic and international instability. Bowling is nostalgic for a lost world before that first major war, for a world in which boys went fishing and their fathers needed no aspirin for frayed nerves. He goes in search of a "settled period . . . when civilisation seems to stand on its four legs like an elephant," when men have a feeling "of not being in a hurry and not being frightened." In such a period the direction in which the future will move—even the need to imagine an after-life—is unimportant, since what is to come is conceived in the image of the contented, unthreatened present.[32]

But in the late thirties, stability has given way to stagnation, and Bowling, like Gordon Comstock, takes a perverse pleasure in imagining his civilization bombed "to hell where it belongs." Part of his resort to imaginary violence comes from his having heard one shoe drop and his waiting impatiently for the other. He listens to a leftist orator arguing British support of Russia against Germany. Stalin, the Red, is "white," but suddenly overnight Hitler, who has been "white," is "black." "But it might just as well be the other way about, because in the little chap's mind both Hitler and Stalin are the same. Both mean spanners and smashed faces."

Bowling is the typical debunking Englishman of the lower classes who has struggled to survive and seemingly has survived to no purpose. He suffers fright, as everyone does, but he is not afraid of the impending war itself. He is afraid of the "after-war."

> The world we're going down into, the kind of hate-world, slogan-world. The coloured shirts, the barbed wire, the rub-

> ber truncheons. The secret cells where the electric light burns night and day [as it does in the Ministry of Love in 1984], and the detectives [or telescreens] watching you while you sleep. And the processions and the posters with enormous faces, and the crowds of a million people all cheering for the Leader till they deafen themselves into thinking that they really worship him, and all the time, underneath, they hate him so that they want to puke. [Winston Smith's "secret loathing of Big Brother" changes helplessly into "adoration" during the two-minutes hate. The woman in front of him breathes "my Saviour" and falls into "prayer."] It's all going to happen. Or isn't it? Some days I know it's impossible, other days . . . inevitable.[33]

Bowling, who in a period of "settled civilisation" would have been content to watch the girls in their summer dresses and the lazy roach in the pool under the willows, has been prodded by events into assuming an attitude toward life that is not only "deeply moral" but political. He fears that decent men like him, "people who *don't* want to go round smashing faces," are in the greatest peril of all because they are politically asleep.

> They can't defend themselves against what's coming to them, because they can't see it, even when it's under their noses. They think that England will never change and that England's the whole world. Can't grasp that it's just a left-over, a tiny corner that the bombs happen to have missed. But what about the new kind of men from eastern Europe, the stream-lined men who think in slogans and talk in bullets? They're on our track. . . . No Marquess of Queensberry rules for those boys. And all the decent people are paralysed. Dead men and live gorillas. Doesn't seem to be anything between.[34]

Although he ends in a stickier domestic glue than Comstock, Bowling has no faith that the British can keep the aspidistra flying. His early vacillation is resolved into the certainty that whether one fights the gorillas or ignores them or joins them, "there's no way out" and the little chaps had better kiss good-bye everything they've known and loved.[35]

Was there no faith equal to fanaticism that, without becoming fanatic in turn, could rally the simple people of the world to defend their liberty, to halt a process which seemed to hurtle them to a doom worse than mere death? One of the things Orwell recalls in "England Your England" is that the little chaps, the Sancho Panzas, the eternal skeptics of any but the most flexible faiths, *could* be heroic, and that while they lacked specific religious beliefs, they were as a whole deeply permeated with "Christian feeling."[36] Their opiates were more likely to be beer and motor cars than any vision of Sugarcandy Mountain in the here-after, and they were unlikely to mistake any of their leaders for saviours. Perhaps there was no single ideology that could take over completely among a people, like the English, so obstinate in clinging to "hobbies," clubs, and private allegiances. The "Christian feeling" of the English may have been no more than a communal obedience of the Golden Rule, a lingering testament of shared humanity, but, Orwell believed, "Nearly everyone, whatever his actual conduct may be, responds emotionally to the idea of human brotherhood."[37]

Winston Smith, to whom Christianity is only a name, intuitively responds to this idea when he thinks of the proles as a great reservoir of sheer animal vitality, life in a kind of undifferentiated protean form, the only form of life that has not substantially changed from what it has always been. It seems to him that by holding on to "primitive emotions" the proles have remained human; they are loyal to human relations, not to the Party. He looks at the grotesque body of the washwoman, deformed by years of child-bearing, by years of unbroken bondage to biologic necessities, engaged in a single, eternal activity of hanging up clothes, and he listens to her song, a parody of his own longing:

> They sye that time 'eals all things,
> They sye you can always forget;
> But the smiles an' the tears acrorss the years
> They twist my 'eartstrings yet!

Smith feels for this woman a "mystical reverence" which is "somehow mixed up with the aspect of the pale, cloudless sky, stretching away behind the chimney pots into interminable distances. It was curious to think that the sky was the same for everybody. . . . And the people under the sky were also very much the same. . . ." [38]

So strong is Smith's response, his innate feeling that this woman and the millions of anonymous proles like her are governed by a law the Party has nothing to do with, a law which decrees a common, everlasting humanity, that against O'Brien's inexorable logic he blurts out his memorable protest: "Somehow you will fail. Something will defeat you. Life will defeat you."

O'Brien upbraids him for naively imagining "that there is something called human nature which will be outraged" by what the Party does and will rise to defeat it. He reminds Smith that the Party *creates* human nature, that men are "infinitely malleable." Does Smith, perhaps, believe in God? No. Then, argues O'Brien, if there is no presiding spirit outside of man which insures human nature and ordains its laws, what does Smith believe can defeat the Party? "I don't know. The spirit of Man." O'Brien then shows Smith his ruined body and tells him mockingly, "If you are human, that is humanity." And Smith, for whom the irony is too much, weeps with "pity for his ruined body." [39]

The scene is especially pathetic because it is inevitable in the condition of mortals that, unless God is in charge of it, the body is the guardian of the human spirit. If its needs are great enough, it can swell up and fill the universe. Before the mind can control the body, the body must be broken. Finally, it is the broken body that controls the mind—the body beyond pain, beyond desire, beyond feeling of any kind.

Smith, of course, is broken because he will not bend, and if the proles in their passive resistance to being dehumanized constitute a tacit challenge to the total power of the Party, this challenge is politically incalculable.

Passive resistance, even when it was employed as a conscious political weapon, seemed to Orwell ineffectual as a means of defeating modern regimes under which opponents of the regimes can be forced to "disappear in the middle of the night." Although Orwell admired Gandhi at least for clearly realizing that one *must* choose sides in a struggle, that is, must be political, he suspected Gandhi's mystique, his political absolute of pacifism, as much as he mistrusted the opposed mystique of power. To oppose power, one had to revert to violence as the only method that had to be met empirically. War might be evil, but it was "an unanswerable test of strength, like a try-your-grip machine." There was "no way of faking the result." [40] What Orwell called "pure" pacifism could appeal only "to people in very sheltered positions." Even then, because it was "negative and irresponsible," he did not believe it could "inspire much devotion." [41]

> Pacifist propaganda usually boils down to saying that one side is as bad as the other, but if one looks closely at the writings of the younger intellectual pacifists, one finds that they do not by any means express impartial disapproval but are directed almost entirely against Britain and the United States. Moreover they do not as a rule condemn violence as such, but only violence used in defence of the Western countries.

Orwell attributes to them a certain Anglophobe relish in seeing their native land humiliated by defeat. They can abjure violence only "because others are committing violence on their behalf." [42] Perhaps in some other world made closer to the heart's desire pacifism might work, but in the modern world otherworldly ideals are inapplicable: "one must choose between God and man."

Even Gandhi's humanistic assumption that all men could be approached by reason, by appeals to common sense and common interest—through "friendly intercourse," that is—even this assumption "is not necessarily true." Reason as an alternative to violence can fail, "for example, when you are dealing with lunatics." [43]

Fanatics of all brands struck Orwell as "lunatics," but political fanatics struck him as by far the most dangerous in his age. He suspected that many of the "revolutionaries" in highly developed countries drew part of their vehemence from a "secret conviction that nothing could be changed." This enabled them, in Britain, for example, to sneer at those who held "the Empire together" and guaranteed them the freedom to be spiteful and at the same time to acquiesce in the exploitation which provided the source of the "family income." These were the very "liberals," Orwell felt, who would become "reactionaries" at the "first brush of reality." [44]

Like Arthur Koestler, whom Orwell sees reflected in his fictitious heroes, the disappointed utopian was liable to turn from necessary political tasks (for example, getting rid of Hitler, which to Orwell seemed a "worthwhile objective," whatever the personal motivation of those who accomplished it: "History has to move in a certain direction, even if it has to be pushed that way by neurotics."). The utopians defaulted because they discovered they could not, merely by disposing of a Stalin or a Hitler, attain perfection in the foreseeable future. Orwell maintains that they were unable to face the possibility that man's problems might never be solved and consequently turned to some "quasi-mystical belief" that "all political action is useless, but that somehow, somewhere . . . , human life will cease to be the miserable brutish thing it now is." [45] In effect, they trusted to miracles rather than to human effort and were ready to swallow whatever the miracle-workers baited the hook with.

Orwell generalizes the "sin of nearly all left-wingers from 1933 onwards": "they have wanted to be anti-Fascist without being anti-totalitarian." Like Koestler, in reaction to the Stalin dictatorship, they retreat into either a "pessimistic Conservatism" or a private absolutism which is no better: quietism and cynicism.[46] They fly from the dream of human justice and liberty straight into the arms of Father State or Mother Church. As Robinson Jeffers says, again in verse, when he coins these epithets, "It is hard to be an adult."

Orwell struggled successfully to avoid the refuge of infantilism. In fact, he stayed a wary distance from parents and gods of any sort. He worshiped neither the false idols of a past glorified by disappointment in the present nor the Bolshevik "saints" whose rule he saw plainly was nothing but a "military despotism enlivened by witchcraft trials."[47] He was a middle man trying to preserve a humane course in the swerving currents of extremism. He was cautious even of proposals which, however sensible in the long run, were for the present political moment not practicable. Of course, he concedes to H. G. Wells, the ultimate solution to jealous and zealous nationalisms is world federation; but, he insists, the "energy that actually shapes the world springs from emotions—racial pride, leader-worship, religious belief, love of war"—feelings which prevail generation after generation mindlessly in the most conservative of political entities: the overwhelming mass of common apolitical men.

Orwell accuses Wells and the "liberal intellectuals" of finding it easy enough to write off feelings as "anachronisms." These theorists have so effectually destroyed strong feelings in themselves "as to have lost all power of action."[48] Orwell knew from his experience in Burma that leadership required a "power of action" and that there was "an appreciable difference between doing dirty work and merely profiting by it."[49] In any successful revolution against tyranny the great, essentially conservative mass would have to be stirred out of their complacence by men, like Wells, who were rich enough to have leisure for general ideas—the leaders would be able to pronounce their aitches—and who *felt* strongly enough to take action at strategic moments.

It was quite likely that theorists who became revolutionary dictators would not do the dirtiest work themselves but make use of the dirtiest fellows to do it. In *1984,* the political prisoners are at the mercy of the most brutish of their fellow prisoners: "positions of trust were given only to the common criminals, especially the gangsters and the murderers, who formed a sort of aristocracy."[50] In a lawless state, where the one unforgivable offense is not murder but "thoughtcrime" and the *sine qua non* of keeping out of prisons is perfection in the process called "crimestop," as Hannah Arendt points out, an early step in killing the "juridical" in man is to convince him, by association with common criminals, of the criminality of his political offense and, by elevating gangsters to a position of trust over him, to convince him that he is the lowest of the low. "Under no conditions," Arendt explains, "must the concentration camp become a calculable punishment for definite crimes." The more "deeply moral" the prisoner, the more profound his moral dislocation. The aim of a totalitarian system is to convert "the whole penal system into a system of concentration camps" for "asocial" elements.[51]

Under a rule of saints, the unorthodox are the "asocial," and total power is the only way to eradicate their "crime." There is an inherent implausibility, then, between the "good" for which power is seized and the means taken to eliminate the "ungood." Theorists who do not suspect the "corrupting effects of power" will commit the most hideous barbarisms in the name of some absolute. Revolutionary dictatorships fail "because of the impossibility of combining power with righteousness." [52]

In theory, the righteous man should be an anarchist. Orwell saw that this was all too easy a refuge. In theory one could conclude, as he did after his Burmese days, "that all government is evil, that the punishment always does more harm than the crime and that people can be trusted to behave decently if only you will let them alone." But if one is an adult, one rejects this theory as "sentimental nonsense. . . . it is always necessary to protect peaceful people from violence. In any state of society where crime can be profitable you have got to have a harsh criminal law and administer it ruthlessly; the alternative is Al Capone." [53]

For this reason—most particularly in a world as yet not governed by universal law, where might is still the judge of right, and international gangsterism supplants even the quasi-honorable old method of alliances and ententes which once balanced power and prevented its *total* abuse—Orwell was suspicious of any theory which holds that right action and good motives in and of themselves, unsupported by laws ruthlessly administered to restrain violence, are sufficient to protect the weak. He could never completely trust *what ought to be* against *what is*—no matter what mystique fostered what pleasant or progressive delusion. Righteousness was the precinct of the saint, and power the precinct of the tyrant.

Ideological thinking, in its compulsion to arrive at a single *total* explanation for all things, necessarily detaches itself from experience as such. It accepts a single categorical imperative upon which to construct a fool-proof system and thereafter discards, ignores, or destroys what is incongruous to that system. It emancipates itself, Arendt says, "from the reality that we perceive with our five senses, and insists on a 'truer' reality. . . ."

> The danger in exchanging the necessary insecurity of philosophical thought for the total explanation of an ideology and its *Weltanschauung*, is not even so much the risk of falling for some usually vulgar, always uncritical assumption as of exchanging the freedom inherent in man's capacity to think for the straightjacket of logic with which man can force himself almost as violently as he is forced by some outside power.[54]

Man can, then, even in the absence of outward compulsion, bring about what Orwell calls a "lunatic dislocation in the mind." He can exchange the empiricism of living for the solipsism of insanity. The assumption that he can thereafter be reached by reason or common sense, by any appeal to pay attention to the world as it is, becomes itself a lunatic assumption. The "pursuit of truth" can drive mankind upon "dark paths of excessive cruelty and of excessive devotion."

Modern man, impatient with the pursuit of something so elusive as to seem non-existent, devises a "perfectionist philosophy" and a totalitarian system to bring the world into line with it. The totalitarian state, Orwell realized, "is in effect a theocracy, and its ruling caste, in order to keep its position, has to be thought of as infallible. But since, in practice, no one is infallible, it is frequently necessary to rearrange past events in order to show that this or that mistake was not made, or that this or that imaginary triumph actually happened."[55] When the delusion of "righteousness," of being in possession of the total truth, combines with total power, the result of course is a delusion of omniscience and omnipotence.

The god who for twenty centuries presided over Western thought created man out of infinite love. God *was* Love. He created because he cared. He was good. In *1984* God is Power, and man is created in his image. The theocracy uncreates what the God of Love created. It dreams, like Milton's Satan, of undoing in a moment what took God six days to make. It is, like Satan, the embodiment of evil, "radical evil," as Arendt calls it, which in our age has "emerged in connection with a system in which all men have become equally superfluous. The manipulators of this system believe in their own superfluousness as much as in that of all others, and the totalitarian murderers are all the more dangerous because they do not care if they themselves are alive or dead, if they ever lived or never were born." [56]

Like Arendt, Orwell saw that today one must choose between the God of Power and Man, must somehow, however futilely, assert the "essence of being human." Otherwise, by 1984 one might be dealing with lunatics, and it might literally no longer make any difference "which side wins." For in the long run a Rule of Saints demands a "schizophrenic system of thought," a disbelief, in fact, in "the very existence of objective truth." [57]

In the 1984 Orwell imagined, war is "abolished," that is, it is perpetual. There is no "least ugly faction" for one to choose.[58] The masses still slumber: they are "free" and their condition is slavery. Outer Party members, if they pray for anything, pray to become perfect in "protective stupidity" and the Inner Party itself is as unapproachable as God in the white cells of its ministries where night and day the light burns and backsliders are made perfect in lunacy. The oligarchy in which power is perpetually guaranteed comprises the most intelligent men, those most adept in doublethink, that is, those in the best position to grasp objective reality and best trained to suppress their knowledge. The demands of their holding power make for a monumental paradox. For example, they are the ones who most firmly and consciously believe that their goal is world conquest and who at the same time understand, in the objective nature of international affairs, that their continuation in power depends upon its not being achieved. In the names of the four great administrative bureaus that have replaced government, the impudent reversal of meaning advertises itself: "The Ministry of Peace concerns itself with war, the Ministry of Truth with lies, the Ministry of Love with torture, and the Ministry of Plenty with starvation." For the achievement of immortality—an achievement which goes against nature—"the prevailing mental condition must be controlled insanity." [59]

The ways of a god have always been inscrutable, and discrepancies between his justice and human ideas of justice have been dismissed by the orthodox as measuring the distance between infinite wisdom and the imperfect wisdom of man. The two, at any rate, *are* incompatible, and one must choose either the inscrutable or the evidence of one's five fallible senses and the "insecurity" of thought.

In *1984* the categorical imperative of the Party is "Reality is only in the mind," and the Party controls or, godlike, "creates" the mind.[60] It can "control" even the laws of nature simply by denying them. It follows then that if O'Brien says to Smith, "You do not exist," Smith is an "unperson." The evidence of his remaining senses, however, as well as his respect for syntax, tell him that O'Brien's statement contains a palpable absurdity. Unless like O'Brien he undergoes a "lunatic dislocation" in his mind, he is a living, if solitary, exception to the absolute. But if a lunatic is "simply a minority of one," if Smith's sense of "reality" is not bolstered by a common sense, then perhaps sanity *is* statistical. In 1984 the "heresy of heresies" is common sense.

The major problem for Smith is, in the absence of any verification whatever, to cling to a faith in his sense of things. What bothers him is not being a lunatic statistically: "the horror was that he might also be wrong."

To fend against this possibility, he himself takes a leap into pure faith: "Truisms are true," he affirms to himself (for he has only, as yet, himself to talk to). "The obvious, the silly, and the true had got to be defended. . . . The solid world exists, its laws do not change. . . . *Freedom is the freedom to say that two plus two make four. If that is granted, all else follows.*" [61] As the night the day, thanks to the spinning earth.

CHAPTER FOUR

THE MINORITY OF ONE

Who alone suffers, suffers most i' th' mind.
—William Shakespeare, "King Lear," III, vi, 110

Every man is a minority of one, a political unit without which democracy is unthinkable. The flesh into which he is locked makes for a kind of inviolable, natural integrity. The flesh may be violated from the ouside: this is the way of power. It may be compelled, subdued, or denied by the mind: this is the way of the saint. Or it may be given: this is the way of love. But a union of any sort—whether it is the "more perfect union" for which government is established, the merging of the 'soul' with an ineffable cosmic spirit, or the 'oneness' of two people in intimacy—presupposes separate and dissimilar members. It presupposes also the insufficiency of "human individuals" to themselves.

Unless he is an eremite seeking union with his god, a human being rarely endures estrangement from his kind for a sustained period without beginning to doubt his sanity. He may choose the solitude of his own company to repair the ravages of social contact, and certain vital activities which no one else can do with him he must necessarily do by himself. (He is inevitably isolated, for example, in pain and in death.) His work may also be done apart from other men; but if that work is not of the world and for the world, if like Gordon Comstock the worker feels a great gulf fixed between what he does and what the world knows of it, he suffers a disintegration of personality which vitiates him precisely as a person aware of his uniqueness *and* his kinship with mankind.

Poverty in a civilized country, Orwell knew, makes a man an outcast, makes it impossible for him to dine with his friends or incur social obligations. His clothes will not bear looking at, he smells bad, and his conversation becomes as impoverished and boring as his existence. Thus cast out from respectable society, a man can at best huddle with other outcasts for animal warmth and dumb sympathy. He lives from hand to mouth, waking only at the insistence of hunger and cold, the urgencies of nature. The outlines of his life lose sharpness, and the future is simply the exigence of the moment he lives into. He stays alive like the proles in *1984*, "against all odds." What he earns is what he must consume; and, when his employment ceases, like the hops-pickers Dorothy Hare works with, he scavenges the countryside like a beast. His toil is sufficient to the day, and he is spared the pain of thought.

If, however, like Rasselas, Johnson's Prince of Abyssinia, his hunger and thirst are effortlessly appeased, he finds that he is not, like a beast, satisfied: "I am, like him, pained with want, but am not, like him, satisfied with fulness." The blissful captive of nature's bounty, he discovers "some latent sense" ungratified or "some desires distinct from sense, which must be satisfied before he can be happy." He walks "burthened" with himself and envies beasts their contentment.[1]

When Dorothy Hare has the misfortune to regain her memory and become a self-sustaining member of society, she is little better than an indentured servant victimized by conditions very much like those against which Winston Smith revolts in *1984*. Her captivity, far from being as "blissful" as Rasselas's, lacks anything to gratify her senses, let alone glut them or even stimulate them. She is dependent for small mercies upon her employer and upon the unalterable nonconformist prejudices of the local P.T.A. for her tenure, which rapidly becomes *un*tenable. Just as she finds a vocation, a mission in life absorbing enough to obviate the physical revulsion which everything else at Mrs. Creevy's establishment inspires in her, her pedagogical heresy is uncovered and rooted out. She is guilty of being happy in her work and of infecting young minds with a love of learning. The old curriculum is imposed with new rigor and, along with it, necessarily, the old discipline. Dorothy learns that "if you are obliged to teach children rubbish, you mustn't treat them as human beings" or they will rebel like human beings. "You must treat them like animals—driving, not persuading. Before all else, you must teach them that it is more painful to rebel than to obey."[2] In other words, you must be—since you have no legitimate *raison d'être*—purely powerful. Your power is the power to make someone else suffer. The powers-that-be in the hierarchy which lowers over Dorothy are intent on destroying the human essence. Since the pleasurable activity of learning keeps it alive against their principles, they degrade Dorothy's teaching to what it *should* be: a joyless, senseless stultification of the young.

Dorothy's lack of privacy under Mrs. Creevy is as oppressive as the loss of her autonomy as a teacher; and paradoxically loneliness—the lack of any kindred soul to talk to—makes even her privacy, when she can steal it, a burdensome, meaningless thing. Diffident by nature and by breeding, she nevertheless finds out, in her loneliness, how fundamentally gregarious she is. She needs others of her kind: "to have at least a home, a family, a few friends who were interested in you!" She pines "for the courage to speak to strangers in the street"; she dreams of getting acquainted somehow with the local vicar for the chance of occupying herself with parish work; sometimes she is so desperate that she thinks of "joining the Y.W.C.A."[3] Lacking a private or domestic realm, Dorothy looks to a public realm where, with others of the human kind, she can appear in word and deed and reaffirm the personality which her role of tyrant in the classroom and of charity ward to Mrs. Creevy has put in doubt. As a mere function in a power structure, she cannot be herself, and deprived of commerce with her kind, she cannot be by herself when she is alone. The mind, she discovers, "will not work to any purpose when it is quite alone." Unable to carry on even the dialogue one has when one talks to oneself, she is nearly out of her mind. Incommunicado, she endures an empty, meaningless cosmos without the power to think of its ramifications.

Once she is rescued from thralldom—and a fairly-tale rescue it is!—once she is returned to the living, her mind recovers its power. Despite his amorous intentions, Warburton is at least someone to talk to. He is eminently verbal and is furthermore well acquainted with the personality Dorothy left behind her in Knype Hill as a memorable, if not brilliant, means of identification.

Unlike Winston Smith, and unlike Warburton, Dorothy has always believed in a benevolent God, at times against indications of His malevolence. It is only when she talks with Warburton that she fully realizes she has lost this belief. Like her faith, her loss of faith is not reasoned; it is purely emotional: "a change in the climate of the mind" wrought imperceptibly by exhaustion, hunger, boredom, frustration, lovelessness, and loneliness.[4] What she has lost is the "power of worship," the impulse to adore, to love unstintingly something commensurate with her emotional capacity.

Faced with Warburton's hedonism and her repugnance to his hairy, satyr-like body, Dorothy has no trouble resisting the life of indolence he holds out to her as an alternative to a bleak spinsterhood in which her time would be divided between placating an irascible, capricious old father and attending to odious, peevish parishioners—a prospect almost unbearable without the comfort of faith. For when, in place of awe, Dorothy endures the "hateful ennui . . . that lies in wait for every modern soul," she first understands what it means to be without faith, without even a mystique of the glands and nerves which continually and subrationally assures her of absolutes good in themselves and immutable. Empty of this assurance, the cosmos is the poorer; everything in it loses lustre and significance.[5]

And yet, what really has changed in the universe? It is "still in a sense the Christian cosmos" Dorothy has always imagined. In God's absence it is governed by the same verities, for the simple reason that those who lose their faith remain, just the same, permeated with Christian feeling. "Beliefs change, thoughts change, but there is some inner part of the soul that does not change. . . ." [6] "Feeling" resists the seduction of ideas, and Dorothy resists the hedonism which seems a plausible enough intellectual alternative. Thankless and arduous as it may be, the "Christian way of life" comes "naturally to her," [7] and she gives herself to effort, to pain, to difficulty rather than to a man who is repugnant to her and a way of life which is alien.

But having made this decision Dorothy does not yet enjoy peace of mind. Like Benjamin, the stoic in *Animal Farm,* she meditates upon the brief passage between womb and tomb and concludes: "in every detail of your life, if no ultimate purpose redeemed it, there was a quality of greyness, of desolation, that could never be described, but which you could feel like a physical pang. . . . Life, if the grave really ends it, is monstrous and dreadful." [8] Only "fools or self-deceivers"—or *rich* hedonists—can face this possibility "without flinching." Without flinching, however, Dorothy faces it and finds no proper "substitute for faith; no pagan acceptance of life as sufficient to itself, no pantheistic cheer-up stuff, no pseudo-religion of 'progress' with visions of glittering Utopias. . . . It is all or nothing. Either life on earth is a preparation for something greater and more lasting, or it is meaningless, dark and dreadful." [9]

Of course, Dorothy is a "no-nonsense" girl and soon chides herself for the theatrical self-pity which proposes these alternatives. Common-sensically she realizes (now that she is home) that her lot is shared by millions of people in the modern world "who had lost their faith without losing their need of faith." [10] Of these millions, there may be thousands who could contrive out of glue and brown paper suits of armor for church pageants no worse than Dorothy's, but Dorothy happens to be the only one in her particular parish who will be bothered.

> Yes here, in this poor, miserable, hampered, despicable Actual, wherein thou even now standest, here or nowhere is

> thy Ideal: work it out thereform; and working, believe, live, be free. Fool! the Ideal is in thyself, the impediment too is in thyself: thy condition is but the stuff thou art to shape that same Ideal out of: what matters whether such stuff be of this sort or that, so the Form thou give it be heroic, be poetic? O thou that pinest in the imprisonment of the Actual, and criest bitterly to the gods for a kingdom wherein to rule and create, know this of a truth: the thing thou seekest is already with thee, 'here or nowhere,' couldst thou only see! . . . . Produce! Produce! Were it but the pitifullest infinitesimal fraction of a Product, produce it, in God's name! 'Tis the utmost thou hast in thee: out with it, then. Up, up! Whatsoever thy hand findeth to do, do it with thy whole might. Work while it is called Today; for the Night cometh, wherein no man can work.[11]

Dorothy is not as long about it as the good Professor Teufelsdröckh, but the similarity of her self-exhortation perhaps justifies his windy intrusion here. Without her precisely recognizing it, the "smell of glue" is the "answer to her prayer." The solution of the problem lies in her tacitly "accepting the fact that there was no solution," no miracle to transform the brutish, miserable thing life is. Dorothy finds that if one simply gets on with "the job that lies to hand" and if that job is "customary, useful and acceptable," the state of one's belief is unimportant. The job at least banishes ennui and makes Dorothy glow—like one beatified—with righteous, unselfconscious sweat. She is simply one of the millions of little people whose inglorious toil is transmuted into something heroic, even poetic, something at least more comely in their condition than Byronic ravings and the delusion that they were born to be happy.

This homely faith in the glue pot, however, presupposes the common light of day before the Night cometh wherein no man can work. It presupposes a human cosmos which, however cruel or meretricious its gods, allows in its huge indifference to them little hovels of personal, useless rubbish to stand, little what-not shelves and anemic aspidistras, little sinecures for clergymen's daughters and bed-ridden aunts, little copses of silver poplars, anonymous havens for lovers and lighted hearths for workmen's families. For, however the tools of work or the machinery of government change, however beliefs and thoughts—the "climate of the mind"—change, some "inner part" of the human soul does not change, and within that part is written the one incorruptible law. Like the coral in the heart of the crystal, it cannot be got at until the crystal itself is smashed. It contains the "essence of being human."

Julia and Smith are confident that nothing will matter, not capture or torture or confession under duress, not even betrayal of each other by word, as long as they are loyal in their hearts: "only feelings matter." Smith tells Julia, "If they could make me stop loving you—that would be real betrayal." Both are sure that the Party "can't get inside you." If you can stay human, you can beat them, and you stay human not in your thoughts, words, or deeds but in the "inner heart, whose workings were mysterious, even to yourself"—that biologically indefinable but undeniable center of man's being where he is impregnable to the "armies of unalterable law" mustered against him.

Julia and Smith speak of their "hearts," the organs of feeling affection for each other. Once declared, this affection unites them; they possess more than the few cubic centimeters in the skull which are the only property of the propertyless in 1984. What each feels in addition to his feeling for the loved one, however, is what Hannah Arendt calls "inwardness as a place of absolute freedom within one's own self," a discovery of fairly recent times as a result of man's "estrangement from the world."

> The experiences of inner freedom . . . always presuppose a retreat from the world, where freedom was denied, into an inwardness to which no other has access. The inward space where the self is sheltered against the world must not be mistaken for the heart or the mind, both of which exist and function only in interrelationship with the world.[12]

One is free only if he can speak and act in the company of peers, in the public space (as Arendt calls it) which in 1984 has been destroyed. What Smith and Julia have, then, is not freedom in any political sense but only the "inner feeling" of freedom which drives them to devise private rules and ultimately to join with The Brotherhood in rebellion.

Because this center of inward freedom inheres in every child born into the world, the only way to abolish it altogether is to destroy the human race. Otherwise men will at least be "alive" and pass on from body to body a vitality the death-wishers do not share and cannot get at. In this sense, Smith is right: the "spirit of man" will defeat the Party, for if it ceases to exist the Party's *raison d'être* ceases with it. So Milton's Death would devour his own mother, Sin, but that he knows, as she explains to Satan, "His end with mine involved." The human spirit, left to itself, sooner or later dispenses with things that serve no purpose. Sin's hungry son acts at least as a sanitation crew for the sinful earth, which would otherwise stink to heaven with corruption; but the Party, having no legitimate governing function, exists solely to render men as superfluous as itself. A society is totalitarian, Orwell writes, "when its structure becomes flagrantly artificial: that is, when its ruling class has lost its function but succeeds in clinging to power by force and fraud." [13]

As Hannah Arendt points out in the opening chapter of *The Human Condition,* with the usurpation of the private and public spheres by the "social," the inner part of the soul which shuns total exposure in the social takes refuge in the intimate and creates its own realm with things that have neither domestic utility nor wordly significance but purely sentimental value. Surrounded by the furniture of this self-created world, the mind turns inward upon its own thoughts and feelings and yearns for someone to share its loneliness. It cries out as Matthew Arnold does in that peculiarly modern poem "Dover Beach,"

> Ah, love, let us be true
> To one another! for the world, which seems
> To lie before us like a land of dreams,
> So various, so beautiful, so new,
> Hath really neither joy, nor love, nor light,
> Nor certitude, nor peace, nor help for pain. . . .

Oceania, assuredly, does not lie before Winston Smith like a land of dreams—not even like a brave new world. The "glittering Utopia" of economic progress, Emmanuel Goldstein explains, has been discredited at precisely the historic point at which technology made it possible. In consequence, the most striking feature of life in 1984 is not "its cruelty and insecurity, but simply its barreness, its dinginess, its listlessness," [14] an intensification of the greyness and desolation Dorothy Hare found palpable in a life without faith. Even Party members live in tenements which were condemned in mid-century and spend their spare time scrounging among the proles for razor blades and shoe strings. The continual internal protest of his viscera persuades Smith that he has "been cheated of something" he has an inalienable right to: "was it not a sign that this was *not* the natural order of things, if one's heart sickened at the discomfort and dirt and scarcity . . . ? Why should one feel it to be intolerable unless one had some kind of ancestral memory that things had once been different?" [15]

It is primarily "feeling" which stimulates Smith to think. In the Ministry of Truth he is employed to rewrite history according to the ideal, that is, according to the Party line of the moment. He realizes that what he does is not even forgery but "merely the substitution of one piece of nonsense for another"; the immorality of his work does not, consequently, bother him. But there is something about not having a past, personal or communal, which terrifies him more than "mere torture and death." If the past does not exist inviolably, regardless of how often it is falsified, then his memory may be no more than a willful hallucination. He has only one clue to his sanity, to the inviolability of the past, to the impossibility that he is "wrong"; once he held in his hands factual corroboration of his own memory of an event. The "memory hole" to which he consigned that evidence is symbolic of the Party's systematic destruction of objective reality, which has always been the test of a man's sanity. The men who "make history" work in the Ministry of Truth, and their product, fittingly enough, is fabrication. The deeds of men are no longer the subject of history. They are literally not *memorable*. Action, in fact, no longer exists. It has been replaced by Physical Jerks, pep rallies, and mass demonstrations.

Following the dictates of his senses, which stubbornly insist that life has not always been as it is under the Party, Smith makes two purchases which, by their presence in the alcove of his room, establish the domain of the intimate. In the "diary," he proposes to address the future, to reach beyond the "locked loneliness" in which he lives to a time when no one will have even his own imperfect memories of the past. He intends to "transfer to paper the interminable restless monologue" which has been going on in his mind for years. But the book he purchases is in excess of what it need be, just as the crystal paperweight is: it is beautiful. It is reminiscent of a time he can only suspect, when it may have been customary for things to be beautiful as well as utilitarian, or merely beautiful for their own sakes, and thus a joy forever. These objects then create, for the purpose toward which Smith's solitary mind works, a symbolic past from which they come and a future into which they will continue meaningfully. Smith's first necessity, in order to think, is to restore time as the abstraction in which men are born, become, and die, producing the infinitesimal fractions which make the world different for their having lived.

Before technological progress was halted, it provided those who rule with the means of perpetual surveillance. Not only then did history stop; "private life came to an end." Under surveillance a man necessarily plays a role. He cannot be himself. His actions are all prescribed. Because he cannot start anything by himself, he is without initiative. He turns to thought, traditionally opposed to action. But in 1984 thought is the "essential" crime that contains "all others in itself," and it is not a crime that can be "concealed forever." Only the "goodthinkful," the purely orthodox, are safe from detection. They know, "without taking thought, what is the true belief or the desirable emotion." The "badthinkful," for fear of being detected, dare not talk to anyone. By keeping everyone continually in the public eye and prescribing the role he must play, the Party successfully isolates him from his kind. The result of togetherness is, ironically, apartness: the cessation of communication—as people gathered together around a television set know.

But even the "goodthinkful" are not as safe as Smith at first supposes. Parsons, who has never sweated an unorthodox drop in his life and who is incapable of thought, betrays his human essence in the final refuge of those who exist altogether under surveillance: sleep. Over and over again he avows his hatred of Big Brother. Syme, the etymologist, in his enthusiasm for Newspeak, betrays a treasonable capacity for passion and a dedication to abstract intellectual matters which emanate from him like a doom. Even Smith intuits directly that "they" will get Syme. And when Smith meets Ampleforth the "poet" in the Ministry of Love and asks him what he is in for, the poet answers, "There is only one offense, is there not?"

"And have you committed it?" Smith asks.

"Apparently I have." [16]

Because there are no laws, men are punished for crimes they have no way of knowing about and no way to keep from committing. The penal system in 1984 is a vast concentration camp in which the punishment for one's crime is incalculable. Until one is apprehended, one lives with an impending sense of evil.

In "Such, such were the joys . . ." Orwell describes the wife of the headmaster at "Crossgates," the name he gives to the school he attended when he was eight years old. "It was very difficult to look her in the face without feeling guilty, even at moments when one was not guilty of anything in particular." [17] The Christian assumption of general guilt in the eyes of the Lord, regardless of one's actual conduct, is enough to make Marlowe's Faustus discard theology—in fact, to throw out the child with the washwater and turn hedonist: "If we say that we have no sin we deceive ourselves and there's no truth in us." And so we sin, and the wages of sin is death. Orwell's particular sin at Crossgates was wetting his bed. Neither terror nor propaganda could prevent him from repeating this offense. Upon being beaten, he cried, but not from the pain.

> I was crying partly because I felt that this was expected of me, partly from genuine repentance, but partly also because of a deeper grief which is peculiar to childhood and not easy to convey: a sense of desolate loneliness and helplessness, of being locked up not only in a hostile world but in a world of good and evil where the rules were such that it was actually not possible for me to keep them.[18]

He sinned not knowing he sinned and not wanting to sin and not being "able to avoid it." With the solipsism of the infant, he understood of the world only that it was inimical to his best intentions. It was impossible in such a world to be good or to hang on to good things. He adopted without question the need to conceal good fortune from the jealous gods who designed the world as a place for suffering.

The pedagogical tactic which prevailed at Crossgates was to make the child feel that, however hard he worked, he could never "make quite the effort . . . demanded." Orwell accepted as gospel the threats of his elders that he was "ruined for life" if he failed to enter a public school and did not consider it incongruous "that the headmaster of a private school should dispose of an army of informers." The headmaster was simply "all-powerful" and his agents were "everywhere." [19] Oceanic society, as Goldstein explains in *1984,* "rests ultimately on the belief that Big Brother is omnipotent and that the Party is infallible." [20]

Orwell found, as time went on, that instead of being grateful to his "benefactors," he hated them; but it was wicked, he perfectly well knew, to hate one's benefactors. He reasoned, understandably, that he was "no good": "I lived among laws which were absolute, like the law of gravity, but which it was not possible for me to keep." [21]

Unlike human laws which are formulated and put on the books by men so that there may be no doubt what constitutes an infraction and what punishment particular infractions entail, such laws lacked consistency with each other and made no reasonable appeal to moral intelligence. They had the gratuitous nature of decrees: they cancelled each other out and yet at any given moment had absolute power over the guilty. They were what Orwell says the doctrines of totalitarianism are: "not only unchallengeable but also unstable. They have to be accepted on pain of damnation, but on the other hand they are always liable to be altered at a moment's notice." [22]

Another educational advantage Orwell enjoyed at Crossgates was "the conviction, so strong in many children, that the things you most want to do are always unattainable." [23] Joys were always forbidden; escapes from surveillance always joyous. The escapes involved a spontaneous rapture in the sensuous: in swimming, running free, reading in sunlit serenity, collecting caterpillars ("the silky green and purple puss-mouth, the ghostly green poplar-hawk"), hunting butterflies, and taking tea "with large slices of pale-coloured cake" at "magic distances" from the school.

But chiefly his schoolday memories are "of squalor and neglect" and of a variety of physical discomforts, not only hunger, cold, disease, and injury but those that offended his sense of personal fastidiousness: the chapped hands and the green scum on one's teeth, the handkerchief "a sodden horror," the dingy, drafty dormitories, the "accumulations of sour porridge" under the rims of the bowls, the slimy plunge bath and "cheesy"-smelling towels. "It is not easy for me to think of my schooldays without seeming to breathe in a whiff of something cold and evil-smelling. . . ." [24]

The difference between school and home was the difference between "reality" and the thing you somehow hadn't to deserve. Home might not be perfect, but it was "ruled by love rather than by fear." Away from home the world was filled with "force and fraud and secrecy," and eventually, against all the instincts of hatred, one found oneself "sucking up" to one's tyrants with "a sort of cringing love"—just as Smith's hatred of Big Brother is converted into abject adoration during the two-minutes hate. "And yet all the while, at the middle of one's heart, there seemed to stand an incorruptible inner self who knew that whatever one did—whether one laughed or snivelled or went into frenzies of gratitude for small favours—one's only true feeling was hatred." [25]

Much of the imaginative material of *1984* obviously came from a mature recall of the life Orwell had unthinkingly felt as a child: "One could do wrong against one's will." There were sins "too subtle to be explained" or "to terrible to be clearly mentioned." A sense of sin was no less strong for one's being totally innocent. One could be made to forget even such a memorable thing as the pleasurable aspect of sexual activity. Dirty words became "abstractly wicked" and were repeated secretly for their "verbal charm" against invulnerable enemies, much as Julia uses them.

Even at an age when the actual terrors had ceased, Orwell remembers, the "official beliefs" formed by them remained unchanged. A child, whose mind works in fearful isolation, Orwell points out, accepts the most patent superstitions as infinite wisdom precisely because what he accepts does not bear scrutiny. He does not perceive that the ideals set before him cancel each other out, that they involve a kind of "doublethink" on the part of the adults who hold them. They are simply the inscrutable. He perceives only that the strong triumph continually over the weak, that life is "hierarchical" and that "whatever happened was right."

Although he accepted the official version of what was "right," Orwell remembers that his "inner self" seemed always "to be awake, pointing out the difference between the moral obligation" demanded by the infallible hierarchy and the "psychological fact" of his existence. One was supposed to love God, but one hated Him. One sympathized intuitively with the victims of His wrath. How "could you love someone whom you feared?" One wished to obey moral injunctions. but one was unable. One took arms against "armies of unalterable law"; consequently one was convinced that "any major undertaking" was foredoomed. Although the "instinct to survive" balanced this "sense of guilt and inevitable failure," it posed a moral problem of its own. To survive with "any kind of independence" meant "breaking rules which you yourself recognized" as absolutes. At the time, Orwell says, "I could not see beyond the moral dilemma that is presented to the weak in a world governed by the strong: Break the rules, or perish. I did not see that . . . the weak have a right to make a different set of rules for themselves." [26]

Later, of course, Orwell did see that in all societies, even those governed constitutionally, "people must live to some extent *against* the existing order." Sancho Panza must sleep (for sleep he will!) with one wary eye open on Don Quixote, who never sleeps unless he is knocked unconscious by a windmill and who feels neither hunger nor pain as a mortal warning. The impulse of Sancho pulls him "in the other direction" instinctively; and Orwell, although he pronounced his aitches, instinctively pulled on Sancho's side.[27]

Orwell's childhood revolt against "unalterable law," he admits, was subrational. He instinctively concealed his feelings from adults, for, unless they seemed ridiculous, they seemed dangerous. The incredible distortions a child is liable to Orwell attributes to its essential loneliness and helplessness. "It neither understands nor questions the society in which it lives, and because of its credulity other people can work upon it, infecting it with the sense of inferiority and the dread of offending against mysterious, terrible laws." [28]

What one needs, when one is a child, is a big brother, a benevolent figure who, initiated already into the mysteries, undertakes one's own initiation, by whatever cruel and necessary means. Big brother is the surrogate, when one is away from home in a place governed by fear and hatred rather than by love, for Mother and Father. He is the intercessor between the eternal and the mortal, between the Ideal and the Actual, between the absolutes of the Father and the erring of the son. He guarantees that the son shall be acceptable to the social family in which all men are brothers, and that as a natural—that is, human—son he shall be brought to love what, in the imperfect state of nature, he unnaturally—that is, humanly—hates.

In *1984,* the Father is the State, and for the first time in the history of the ill-run race, the State has the means (the "priests of power") of enforcing complete obedience to its will, that is, "complete uniformity of opinion on all subjects."[29] Big Brother is merely the "guise in which the Party chooses to exhibit itself to the world," since the god it serves is inscrutable. Below Big Brother in the hierarchy come the Inner Party and the Outer Party. Party unity is assured by adherence to a common ideology. Unlike hereditary monarchies of the past and like, for example, the Catholic Church, the Party is an adoptive institution. The ideological uniformity of its members makes any particular member superfluous and the Party itself self-perpetuating, very much like an organism which lives eternally like the jellyfish, simply by replacing cells. The essence of Party rule is "the persistence of a certain world view and a certain way of life, imposed by the dead upon the living. . . . *Who* wields power is not important, provided that the hierarchical structure remains always the same."[30] The basis of the hierarchy is, of course, ignorance and poverty.

Those who, at any given moment, wield power, the new oligarchy founded on ideological orthodoxy alone, are, unlike the governing groups of the past, not tempted by the incidental perquisites of power but by the thing itself. The power of the Party is absolute in so far as it controls totally the reality human consciousness embraces. Reality in 1984, as O'Brien assures Winston Smith, exists not faultily in individual minds susceptible to aberration but securely in the great "collective mind" of the Party. Because the Party perpetually succeeds itself, it is immortal; and because it is immortal the truths in its collective mind at any given moment are absolute truths. Because these truths are guaranteed in perpetuity, those in power care no more than saints whether they live or die. The "collective solipsism" of the Party denies objective reality much as the saint negates life as a valley of shadows. The world and the human beings in it are alike superfluous. God is the only reality, and God is Power.

With just his unassisted ingenuity to guide him, Winston Smith has tried to imagine why the Party takes such pains to create a reality contradicted at every point by empirical assessment, why the "huge imposture" is undertaken. His imagination is winningly old-fashioned. Like a latter-day Mandeville, he reasons that the Party justifies its existence by proposing to relieve mankind once and for all of the difficult choice between slavery and freedom. It *is* hard to be an adult. He expects O'Brien to explain that the fallible masses, like children, don't know what is best for them, that the Party in its superior wisdom works for the good of the majority: "That the Party was the eternal guardian of the weak, a dedicated sect doing evil that good might come, sacrificing its own happiness to that of others."

Even such homiletic hypocrisy would be comforting in comparison with what O'Brien actually tells him. O'Brien understands the incompatibility of "righteousness" and "power."

> The Party seeks power entirely for its own sake. We are not interested in the good of others; we are interested solely in power. Not wealth or luxury or long life or happiness; only power, pure power.

Unlike the oligarchies of the past who deceived themselves and their followers into believing that they would wield power only until an earthly paradise was achieved, the Party knows what it is doing, knows that no one ever seizes power with the idea of relinquishing it.

> Power is not a means; it is an end. One does not establish a dictatorship in order to safeguard a revolution; one makes a revolution in order to establish the dictatorship. The object of persecution is persecution. The object of power is power. . . . power is collective. The individual only has power in so far as he ceases to be an individual.[31]

Alone and free, man is doomed and defeated. He has only as much manpower—that is, native strength—as the next individual in his species. He is the victim of his very individualism; he has always in the end to succumb to the condition of

being human, which is to die. His only salvation
self-abnegation, in losing his precious identity and beco
cell in a man-made organism which is eternally self-rep
ing. There his power is the power of submerged identities, the power even Parson's children can wield: the power over other human beings, which is enjoyed consciously only when those human beings suffer. Progress, then, is not an advance toward equality and justice but toward increasing pain. Pain can make a man think of nothing but himself. He can wish only that it should stop. If the world is not witness to his suffering, if it inspires no one else to take up his cause, why should he martyr himself for the sake of an arithmetic equation? If one is quite alone in the truth, one's mind works to no purpose. Smith discovers to his relief that when O'Brien holds up four fingers he can force himself to see five. It does not require infinite pain for Smith to abdicate the mind; yet O'Brien promises that pain will increase until it fills the universe. The commandment of God is no longer "Love thy neighbor as thyself" but "Cause thy neighbor to suffer even as thou suffereth." In this regard, the "old civilizations claimed that they were founded on love and justice. Ours is founded upon hatred. In our world there will be no emotions except fear, rage, triumph, and self-abasement. Everything else we shall destroy. . . ." [32]

O'Brien's explanation of the "why" of the tremendous imposture comes in the second stage of Smith's purification, the stage of "understanding." Characteristically, the answer to Smith's sensible question is insane, that is, it answers nothing: the "intoxication of power" exists in order to eradicate everything but the "intoxication of power." The answer typifies the "lunatic dislocation in the mind" which frightens Smith more—as a possibility deliberately realized—than O'Brien's charge that he alone is "mentally deranged." Smith is in the Ministry of Love to be re-deranged; he is finally in the place of everlasting (artificial) light, in the place where there is no darkness and where hope of anything but perfect orthodoxy must be abandoned by all who enter. "What can you do," Smith thinks, "against the lunatic who is more intelligent than yourself, who gives your arguments a fair hearing and then simply persists in his lunacy?"[33]

The divine light of reason given to man to insure his moral being, that "virtuous light," as Elinor Wylie calls it, has been snuffed out in O'Brien.

> A private madness has prevailed
> Over the pure and valiant mind;
> The instrument of reason failed
> And the star-gazing eyes struck blind.
>
> Sudden excess of light has wrought
> Confusion in the secret place
> Where the slow miracles of thought
> Take shape through patience into grace.
>
> Mysterious as steel and flint
> The birth of this destructive spark
> Whose inward growth has power to print
> Strange suns upon the natural dark.

And, locked in the flesh, Smith's mind is dominated by the single *sensation* of pain.

> O break the walls of sense in half
> And make the spirit fugitive!
> This light begotten of itself
> Is not a light by which to live!
>
> —Elinor Wylie, "O Virtuous Light"

The "walls of sense" which house the spirit ordinarily protect the mind against its self-begotten aberrations by reporting through sight, hearing, smell, taste, and touch an empirical sense of the world. Nothing is so but thinking makes it so, and to Smith in the Ministry of Love the flesh is a prison. Suffused with pain, it fills the universe, crowding the pitiful truths he vowed to defend to the periphery of consciousness. Unconsciousness, the death of the senses, would seem the only refuge. Yet even the disembodied Belial, tormented ceaselessly in Milton's Hell by a pain designed specifically for "celestial essences," dreads the oblivion which attends the cessation of pain:

> . . . for who would lose,
> Though full of pain, this intellectual being,
> Those thoughts that wander through eternity . . . ?
>
> —*Paradise Lost,* II, 146–48

Rather than defy God outright, Belial thinks to placate Him with a show of self-abnegation, reserving in the inner part of his being the evil for which he has been damned. Similarly, Smith experiments with the behavior his tormentor requires. For a "fleeting instant" he acquiesces to bodily pain and enjoys, with the lapse of conscious control, the "luminous certainty" that O'Brien's four fingers are five—a strange sun printed on the natural dark! "Then everything was normal again, and the old fear, the hatred, and the bewilderment came crowding back again." [34]

When Smith reaches a stage of mental disability, when he realizes the "arithmetical problems raised, for instance, by such a statement as 'two and two make five' [are] beyond his intellectual grasp," he understands what the initiate into doublethink needs to understand: his helpless ignorance. He must develop from scratch a mental athleticism which requires simultaneously the "most delicate use of logic" and unconsciousness of the "crudest logical errors." Stupidity, he learns, is "as necessary as intelligence, and as difficult to attain." [35]

But Smith is at last willing to try what is required. He is in a Lord-I-believe-help-thou-my-unbelief frame of mind. He falls into a "blissful reverie" of anticipating the time when everything will come clear, when not only pain and fear will vanish but the doubts and arguments which have made them necessary. Relaxing his vigilance, he dreams of the Golden Country and discovers that Julia is "not merely with him" as a distinct, separable entity "but inside him." He knows what Belial should know, that there is no concealing what lies in the heart, that "if you want to keep a secret you must also hide it from yourself"— from that interminable monologist which articulates private feelings even in those who claim not to be conversant with them.

> In the old days he had hidden a heretical mind beneath an appearance of conformity. Now he had retreated a step further: in the mind he had surrendered, but he had hoped to keep the inner heart inviolate. He knew that he was in the wrong, and he preferred to be in the wrong. . . . From now onwards he must not only think right; he must feel right, dream right. And all the while he must keep his hatred locked up inside him like a ball of matter which was part of himself and yet unconnected with the rest of him, a kind of cyst.[36]

In thought, then, Smith is almost perfect: he knows what has to be done. O'Brien commends him and says, "It is only emotionally that you have failed to make progress." It is not enough to obey Big Brother: "you must love him." And since Smith's hatred is a malignancy which is not self-operable, the Ministry of Love has lovingly devised the cure: "a form of pressure that you cannot withstand, even if you wished to. You will do what is required of you." [37]

Faced with the rats, Smith finds himself "in the middle of a great empty plain, a flat desert drenched with sunlight," the Golden Country stripped of distracting sensory features and of human companionship. He knows he must "interpose another human being, the *body* of another human being, between himself and the rats"; and since Julia is "inside him" he sacrifices her body as she sacrifices his. Later when the two of them meet, there is a mute exchange: This is my body, broken for you.

Orwell ironically echoes the ancient mystique of salvation. Christ, the intercessor between the Father and Old Adam, interposed his body between the blinding light of the all-powerful and the endless darkness of perdition. His sacrifice, the flesh given in love, was the prerequisite exacted by the Father for disobedience, the price to be paid for a more perfect love and a peace that surpassed "understanding."

Even as Smith undergoes the second phase of his initiation

into Party mysteries, whether O'Brien is a friend or a foe does not seem to matter. He is, Smith feels, someone to talk to, someone who, by understanding his heresies even before he utters them, is virtually omniscient. Until he emerges "cured" from Room 101, Smith's greatest fear is that O'Brien will convert him. He feels between himself and this inner-sanctum Party member a peculiar bond of humanity, something inherent in their given nature which cannot be gainsaid. "In some sense that went deeper than friendship, they were intimates," and Smith has, waking and sleeping, dreamed of a place, somewhere out of this world, "where they could meet and talk." [38]

But the outcome of their "talk" exceeds Smith's imaginative bounds. He can barely tolerate the alternative his dread invents: that if the powers-that-be have converted O'Brien to their species of insanity they can convert him too. For O'Brien seems to Smith an unlikely candidate for fanaticism; he has none of the stupidity and single-mindedness that characterize the most orthodox Party members. When Smith launched upon his solitary revolution against the Party, when he "moved from thoughts to words" and then from "words to action," he clasped O'Brien's hand in ignorance of whether he was friend or foe, in darkness, in intuitive, personal brotherhood. And O'Brien told him at that time that The Brotherhood could never be destroyed because it did not exist as an organized body like the Party, but consisted of individuals working in the dark unknown to each other, sustained merely by an idea which is indestructible, with only the hope that they could "extend the area of sanity little by little." The Brotherhood, then, is sustained by a degree of belief that amounts to mysticism.

Perhaps the most terrifying possibility in *1984* is one which Orwell leaves implicit in the situation: there can never be any way of knowing that O'Brien is not at one and the same time a Party member of perfect orthodoxy and a member of The Brotherhood. For all practical purposes it simply does not matter. This possibility, though not explicit in anything Orwell says about O'Brien, signifies the ultimate meaninglessness and hopelessness of modern man's alternatives. Smith has sworn, in the cause of brotherhood, to resort to every foul trick the enemy uses. In volunteering to deceive, bully and kill, he promises to suspend the moral faculties of compassion and judgment. The Brotherhood is more than likely sponsored by Big Brother himself as a means of decoying anyone animated by notions of founding society on love and justice, but one cannot be sure. In the very nature of The Brotherhood, which is conspiratorial, brother can never stand forth in the light and stand by his brother. Loyalty to the cause takes precedence over love of individuals. Human solidarity, which alone convinces the mind that its truths are worth fighting for, is consequently sacrificed to expedience. The catechism of the revolutionary is a declaration of irresponsibility in the use of power to achieve one's ends. Only power can challenge power. An idea may be indestructible, but until it is enacted it is impotent.

Smith, then, even before his "cure" in the Ministry of Love, is potentially indistinguishable from his enemies, just as the O'Brien who sacrifices his brother for the cause of brotherhood is indistinguishable from the Grand Inquisitor of the Party. Thanks only to Julia's impetuous refusal in O'Brien's apartment the night the two of them take their oath of loyalty to The Brotherhood, Smith has not pledged to set loyalty to a cause higher than love. O'Brien knows, then, that in the "inner self" these two cling to the ultimate heresy and can be trusted as little for revolutionary as for Party purposes.

Julia and Smith are apprehended in the realm of the intimate, the odor of Julia's scent and of real "free-market" coffee filling the air they breathe. They have plugged one rat hole but never suspected where the rats really are: behind the old, cherished print on the wall. Smith's diary, as well as Julia's note and the secret corroboration of his sanity which Smith thought he destroyed, have been confiscated by the Thought Police and converted into exhibits of their guilt. Prophetically, the crystal is smashed on the hearthstone. Against omniscience, the heart has no secrets. Against omnipotence, the individual will is nil.

In the first stage of initiation, the flesh is violated: Smith "learns" that it is less painful to obey than to rebel. In the second stage, he "understands" the power of the mind over the report of the senses: two fingers and two fingers equal five unfingers. In the final stage, he wins the victory over his inner self and is suffused with love for Big Brother. He is saved from the pain of living and being human and guaranteed immortality. The poetic justice of it is almost beautiful; for the "essence of being human," as Orwell says, is "that one is prepared in the end to be defeated and broken" as the "inevitable price of fastening one's love upon other human individuals." Big Brother, however, is a "guise" and can be loved without the "hard work" human love entails. Now that Smith is superfluous, unfit for work of any kind, he plays with himself a game of chess, just a "temporary and local phase in an enormous game . . . being played over the whole surface of the earth," a game in which good unvaryingly triumphs.[39]

Because no man is an island unto himself, every man's death entails the extinction of an irreplaceable uniqueness and the diminution of human solidarity; for one's belief in the world of solid objects and one's belief that man is noble and life worth living are immeasurably strengthened by being shared. In his early piece "A Hanging," Orwell remembers the dog which bounded forward into the hanging party, "wagging its whole body." The hangmen were "aghast," for the dog was "wild with glee at finding so many human beings together." When the prisoner on his way to be hung fastidiously avoided a puddle in his path, Orwell for the first time became aware of "what it means to destroy a healthy, conscious man." He saw

> the mystery, the unspeakable wrongness, of cutting a life short when it is in full tide. This man was not dying, he was alive just as we are alive. All the organs of his body were working—bowels digesting food, skin renewing itself, nails growing, tissues forming—all toiling away in solemn foolery. . . . His eyes saw the yellow gravel and the gray walls, and his brain still remembered, foresaw, reasoned—reasoned even about puddles. He and we were a party of men walk-

> ing together, seeing, hearing, feeling, understanding the same world; and in two minutes, with a sudden snap, one of us would be gone—one mind less, one world less.[40]

The tragedy of Winston Smith is more, however, than the destruction of a healthy, conscious man; it is the tragedy that inheres in the extinction of a species. The tragedy no longer touches Smith, who in the end is gathered happily to the bosom of his makers; but the sense of tragedy, as Orwell conjectures, may be incompatible with a belief in God and be lacking in anyone who comes to regard human beings as superfluous. At any rate, Orwell asserts, the sense of tragedy "is not compatible with disbelief in human dignity and with the kind of 'moral demand' which feels cheated when virtue fails to triumph. A tragic situation exists precisely when virtue does *not* triumph but when it is still felt that man is nobler than the forces which destroy him." [41] Thus it is that Winston Smith's tragedy touches us.

CHAPTER FIVE

THE GOLDEN COUNTRY

. . . that sweet golden clime.

—William Blake, "Ah Sunflower! Weary of Time"

Whoever knows the source of Orwell's title "Such, such were the joys . . ." suspects his affinity for William Blake, an affinity Orwell alludes to himself in confessing, in "Why I Write," that his first memorable metaphor at the age of four or five (a tiger with "chair-like teeth") was quite possibly a "plagiarism of Blake's 'Tiger, Tiger.' "

There is something in Orwell of Blake's Isaiah, the prophet who, admitting that he neither saw nor heard God "in a finite organical perception," nevertheless was firmly persuaded *by his senses* "that the voice of honest indignation is the voice of God" and so "cared not for consequences, but wrote."

Isaiah's interlocutor asks: "does a firm perswasion that a thing is so, make it so?"

"All poets believe that it does," Isaiah answers, "& in ages of imagination this firm perswasion removed mountains; but many are not capable of a firm perswasion of anything." In Orwell's words, they have never felt strongly tempted to be human.

For all their unheroic qualities—perhaps accounting for them—Orwell's fictitious characters have in common a generous capacity to be firmly persuaded by their senses. Dorothy, early in her story, oppressed by the prospect of pleading with tradesmen, by the tedium of parish calls, and by the immediate horror of having to succeed Miss Mayfill at the communion chalice, catches sight through the open church door of the earth illuminated by a sunburst.

> . . . some jewel of unimaginable splendour had flashed for an instant . . . and then faded. . . . The flash of living colour had brought back to her, by a process deeper than reason, her peace of mind, her love of God, her power of worship. Somehow, because of the greenness of the leaves, it was again possible to pray. O all ye green things upon the earth, praise ye the Lord! [1]

Later the same morning she is again "overwhelmed" and "dizzied" by the sensuous beauty of the earth; she feels a "mystical joy" in the "very nature of things" which she mistakes for love of God. The "lovely scent" of summer days, the vibrant mingling of sounds like a "mighty anthem of Praise," the mere sight of the land sunning itself—all move her to such ardent worship that she kisses the fennel against her face and suddenly realizes that her senses have betrayed her into a "half-pagan ecstasy."

In *Burmese Days* Flory is similarly caught off guard during a tramp he has undertaken as a therapeutic for the ennui and futility of his existence. He has earnestly, but of course secretly, yearned (as Comstock and Bowling yearn) for some sort of violence to shatter life's stagnation: a native uprising. Yet, in his inner heart, he knows he does not sincerely care if the English are despotic. His longing for a change in the political climate is actually a longing for a change in the "climate of the mind." The unwritten censorship code which demands, among the Anglo-Indians, perfect conformity of opinion—even a peculiar jargon in which to couch opinions —has effectually deprived Flory of "the right of free speech" and any honest commerce with his kind. He has in self-defense developed an inward life which no one shares but Dr. Veraswami, whom he argues with as he might argue with himself. As he cools his body in an isolated pool, he is smitten by the exquisite coloring of a pigeon over his head.

> A pang went through Flory. Alone, alone, the bitterness of being alone! So often like this, in lonely places in the forest,

> he would come upon something—bird, flower, tree—beautiful beyond all words, if there had been a soul with whom to share it. Beauty is meaningless until it is shared. If he had one person, just one, to halve his loneliness! [2]

His only hope of escaping from the prison of himself is to find a secret sharer of his terrible ambivalence toward life. Failing that in the end and finding at hand no tool conformable to his hand except a gun, he understandably, if melodramatically, shoots himself—having just put down a native insurrection and having been publicly disgraced by the Burmese mistress whom he has treated worse than his dog.

George Bowling, an unlikely character for this sort of thing, is all the same possessed of some vestigial organ which, despite the artificial insularity of his life, registers change of season—"God, what a day!" The primroses are out and the weather is "too good to miss." Bowling leaves the protection of his car and goes after some primroses with the faded notion of gathering them while he may. He finds himself completely alone, a situation which, because the world is too much with him, makes him inexplicably happy. Something—perhaps no more than "seasonal effect on the sex-glands"—suddenly convinces him that life is "worth living." The red embers under the ash of a tramp's abandoned fire give him a "feeling of life" more intense and vibrant than Bowling can quite find words for, but it assures him that, like the embers, he is alive under the dull ash. He removes his false teeth and assesses his physical and domestic stock—nothing to brag about; and yet he is suffused with a "peaceful feeling" which he likens to a guarded inner flame. He is through with ambition, he is through with women. To all intents and purposes he has nothing to live for, and, even if he had, the gorilla hordes are about to smash it. Yet in that one moment, "looking at the primroses and the red embers under the hedge," he does not pine for rejuvenation: "I only want to be alive."

In this mood he rejects the idiocies of civilized people and considers it sufficient that in the nearby pool the infinite mystery of life lies open to man's curiosity. The water creatures, visible and invisible, exist eternally the same, whatever man does. Bowling blesses them unaware: "You could spend a lifetime watching them, ten lifetimes, and still you wouldn't have got to the end even of that one pool. And all the while the sort of feeling of wonder, the peculiar flame inside you. It's the only thing worth having. . . ." The peace Bowling experiences has nothing to do with his country's being, at the moment, technically at peace. It is a "feeling in your guts. And it's gone for ever if the rubber truncheon boys get hold of us."

Pursued by the imaginary disapproval of "people whom you've never seen but who rule your destiny all the same, the Home Secretary, Scotland Yard, the Temperance League, the Bank of England, Lord Beaverbrook, Hitler and Stalin on a tandem bicycle, the bench of Bishops, Mussolini, the Pope. . . ."[3] Bowling takes his final fling at life; but it is not the lost weekend of a man whose quiet desperation erupts uncontrollably into noisy desperation. Without its pathos, Bowling's search resembles Willy Loman's directionless probe of the past for something that retains meaning and value. His search for the peace of a settled time is symbolized by his effort to locate the deep pool filled with ancient, placid carp which in his boyhood Bowling discovered, a secret pool which still seems to be his if he can get back to it. Its location is less geographical than psychological. It lies in a golden country where summer is eternal and even adults are children in their contentment with simple things. Perhaps the only verse approaching poetry that Orwell ever wrote memorializes the dilemma of modern man as he saw it and his own dilemma as he felt it and bestowed it on Bowling. Harassed by an uncongenial world, he yearns for a land of love and warm days;

> But girls, bellies and apricots,
> Roach in a shaded stream,
> Horses, ducks in flight at dawn,
> All these are a dream.[4]

Knowing it is a dream, Bowling nevertheless tries to recapture the innocence of sensory joys and the honesty of simple people. He finds his pool converted into a rubbish dump in a real estate development of sham Tudor dwellings the inmates of which (dietary fadists intent on getting back to Nature en masse) have the disadvantage of not being, like the inmates of the insane asylum which once stood on their property, decently locked up.

The impossibility of hanging onto dreams and the actual evil that may attend converting dreams into actualities (Lenin, like Major in *Animal Farm,* after all, had a vision and made the mistake of acting on it) do not condemn dreams as such. People may lose their dreams, as they lose their faith, but they do not lose their *need* for dreams. Like childhood, dreams exist inviolably in a region not accessible to adults—or revealed to them only in the flash of a bird's wing, in unexpected moments of tenderness, in unbidden images out of the past, like the song which Major remembers from his youth. The melody is always familiar, but the words are elusive. They were sung "long ago and have been lost to memory for generations." Bowling sensibly concludes that there is no revisiting boyhood scenes. There is no "air" a poor fish can come up for. The earth is still vast, but man has dirtied most of it.

Sometimes memory is so submerged that one must begin, simply as Winston Smith begins, to rely on a sixth sense, on the firm persuasion of one's "skin" and "stomach" that the present "texture of life" is an outrage; to be convinced that the voice of honest indignation is the voice of God; to care not for consequences but to do as Smith does: write. His first entry in the seditious diary is a declaration of independence: "DOWN WITH BIG BROTHER." Then, knowing that he will perish, whether or not he breaks the rules of the strong, he devises a political axiom by which he will be ruled—knowing also that if he cannot keep alive the mind as the proles keep alive the body truth will perish with him: *"Freedom is the freedom to say that two plus two make four. If that is granted, all else follows."*

What Smith most wants to preserve for the future, however, is not an arithmetic equation but a felt truth that almost defies articulation. Deeply buried as it is, a memory rises irrepressibly in Smith's dreams. It reveals a landscape expressive of an "ancient time . . . when there were still privacy, love, and friendship," a time before emotion lost its dignity and sorrows their depth and complexity, a time in which tragedy was still possible. The name *Shakespeare* comes to Smith like an unvindicated ghost from an ancestral memory that twists him and tangles him witlessly in nostalgia. Tragedy—the eternal story of man's being, in the end, broken by life as the price he pays for being human. Dim, half-submerged remembrances of times past—some of them tinged with guilt (one imperfectly recalled image of an infinitely gentle, infinitely suffering thing which he betrayed long ago)—are no more than hints of a personal biography and are dimmed by the bold gesture of sexual defiance the dark-haired girl makes in his dream. But Smith clings to these images because, without external records, the outline of his life loses form and thus significance.

It is some time before these images come completely into focus for Smith, not until his intuitive belief in them has determined his future; but it is not long before the brilliant and frightening premonition of Julia is made actual by her declaration of independence, her word committed dangerously to paper: "I LOVE YOU."

Love is the private rule of the apolitical individual weak in the isolation of his flesh against the massed strength of a multi-cellular body moved by hatred. For Orwell, as for Blake, the earth slept in darkness, nurturing the undifferentiated capacities for love, sorrow, and courage, long-suffering even in sleep but at least, because unconscious, not liable to beget upon itself the "excess of light" that meant madness, the repressive, restrictive "reason" which hypocritically justified slavery and joylessness. For Orwell and for Blake, God is Love, and—as the Devil in Blake's *The Marriage of Heaven and Hell* angers the orthodox angel by proclaiming—"The worship of God is: Honouring his gifts in other men, each according to his genius, and loving the greatest men best: those who envy or calumniate great men hate God; for there is no other God." The "Divine Image" is man's. His body is the form divine manifesting God's attributes: "Love, Mercy, Pity, Peace." All "must love the human form," said Blake, who never told lies in prose.[5]

If pain causes a man to sense nothing but himself, pleasure requires him to sense something besides himself.[6] The one thing above all others which is not beautiful until it is shared is sexual pleasure, a worship, so to speak, of God incarnate in the "human form divine," which is capable without thought of the most intense—and also the most perishable—of raptures. Unlike Smith, who formulates his rebellion against ideological insanity, Julia is a rebel only "from the waist downwards." The difference between truth and falsehood, so important to Smith, simply doesn't interest her. Her ignorance is her strength. She knows instinctively that Party propaganda is all sham and cares only to outwit the Party as a natural, implacable enemy. Her philosophy is as simple as that of a child at "Crossgates": you wanted to have a good time and "they" wanted to stop you. "The clever thing was to break the rules and stay alive all the same." If you kept the small rules, you could break the big ones with impunity, she argues.

The ultimate goal of the Party is to supplant pleasure with pain: "We shall abolish the orgasm!" O'Brien shrieks in his peroration. The Party tolerates debauchery, so long as it is "furtive and joyless. . . . The aim of the Party was not merely to prevent men and women from forming loyalties which it might not be able to control. Its real, undeclared purpose was to remove all pleasure from the sexual act. Not love so much as eroticism was the enemy, inside marriage as well as outside it."[7]

Julia's promiscuity, the form her rebellion takes, is precisely what Smith loves most: she loves, not just him, but the thing itself. She loves love as O'Brien loves power. Because everything, with Julia, comes "back to her own sexuality," she divines the "direct, intimate connection between chastity and political orthodoxy" much more swiftly than Smith. She simply knows it in her bones: "If you're happy inside yourself, why should you get excited about Big Brother and the Three-Year Plans and the two Minutes Hate and all the rest of their bloody rot?" [8] Without the least interest in politics as such, Julia has a radical understanding of the Party's "puritanism." She opens Smith's eyes to the political potential not only of economic and social privation but of sexual starvation: it induces an hysteria which can easily "be transformed into war fever and leader worship."

From Julia there breathes, as there breathes from Ravelston's rich, insouciant mistress, "a powerful wordless propaganda against all altruism." [9] The demands of her body insure a solipsistic arrangement of the world to satisfy desire. Driven to formulate her promiscuity as politically significant, Smith is comforted to think that Julia is not impelled by the "love of one person" so much as by "animal instinct" and that such "simple undifferentiated desire" should be sufficient to "tear the Party to pieces." With no real grasp of Party ideology and its ramifications in the abstract, Julia presents the appearance of unblemished orthodoxy, as naturally as a salamander takes on protective coloring. Watching her fall asleep whenever he discourses on doctrine, Smith realizes that "the world-view of the Party"—that is, what it substitutes for government and politics—imposes itself "most successfully on people incapable of understanding it . . . By lack of understanding they remained sane." Simple bodily desire, then, which sometimes resists the harshest conditioning, seems to Smith an innate guarantee that the Party will be defeated by "Life." Desire, he decides, is in effect thoughtcrime in a Party member, the essential crime that contains all others; and copulation, successfully—that is, joyously—completed, is a "blow struck against the Party . . . a political act." Pure love, pure desire, without political consequence, has become as obsolete as "ownlife"; for "the sex instinct created a world of its own which was outside the Party's control and which therefore had to be destroyed."

Eroticism, attended or not by gentler, connubial feelings, is in *1984* the mindless life force the hardiness of which is manifest in Julia, an Anti-Sex Leaguer in good standing. It is the means of man's achieving by his own unassisted will an extension of his strength in the singular. The object of eroticism is never consciously to "make a baby," although the making of babies has, from time out of mind, perpetuated individual men and women in the immortal life of their species. "Making a baby" in 1984 is synonymous with doing "one's duty to the Party" (the phrase has a perfidious, obscene ring to it), replenishing a cell in an enormous organism which is teleologically defunct in that its sole goal is to destroy what makes human life significant. The labor of "making a living" and the labor of "making a baby," the kinds of labor peculiar to each sex, both of which entail pain, remain in 1984 with much the punitive effect of the original edict for the "forms divine" once they had fallen from innocence. But the compensatory pleasures of "making love" and "making a home" where love rules instead of fear are rigidly proscribed. Because Julia and Smith love each other they can never form an indissoluble union.

There comes a time when Smith desires nothing more than being alone with Julia *free* of the political compulsion to make love. Frustrated one night by a natural obstacle to love-making which the Party has seen no reason to tamper with, Smith is at first angry, then quickly repentant and overwhelmed by a tenderness for Julia quite free of sexuality. He is filled with domestic yearnings. The age-old pleasures of family and hearth are more unobtainable than razor blades and shoe laces. But Smith wishes ardently that he and Julia were an old married couple, walking together "openly and without fear, talking of trivialities and buying odds and ends for the household," enjoying not a political triumph but the simple joys that are available to Gordon Comstock once he abandons his futile rebellion against the money-god. Moved by this longing, Smith takes a step as irrevocable as opening the diary: he contracts for a hovel among the proles for the specific indulgence in "ownlife" which neither he nor Julia has ever known. Here, like the new and old worlds of ancient history, each is a world and hath a world, seemingly apart from the world the Party controls. Here their waking souls

. . . watch not one another out of fear;
For love all love of other sights controls,
And makes one little room an everywhere.[10]

—John Donne, "The Good-morrow"

Here they lie on the lumpy, bug-infested mattress, making love when they want to, not when they have to, hearing the shouts of prole children and the interminable song of the washwoman in the near distance, a song filled with a "happy melancholy" which expresses Smith's mood. He longs for this life as a normal experience. If it were, he would be content just to be alive. He would care no more about overthrowing the Party than Flory cares about the Burmese taking back their country. "The paperweight was the room he was in, and the coral was Julia's life and his own, fixed in a sort of eternity at the heart of the crystal." [11]

Party members, Winston muses, as he listens to the shoddy but somehow beautiful song of the woman below, never sing. In them, singing would seem "slightly unorthodox, a dangerous eccentricity, like talking to oneself," something with an old-fashioned charm like the cosmetics Julia has used to enhance her femininity, like the aroma of real coffee and the silky texture of real sugar—for that matter, like some of O'Brien's mannerisms, as he, for example, adjusts his eyeglasses—or like the verses about the bells of St. Martin's. These things are beautiful in themselves and for themselves, like the thrush in the wood which sang (perhaps into a hidden microphone) when

So little cause for carollings
  Of such ecstatic sound
Was written on terrestrial things
  Afar or nigh around
That I could think there trembled through
  His happy goodnight air
Some blessed Hope, whereof he knew
  And I was unaware.[12]

—Thomas Hardy, "The Darkling Thrush"

In an effort to assuage his starved senses, Smith has searched for Beauty as well as Truth. Because it is "a beautiful thing" he risks owning the glass globe. ("Anything old, and for that matter anything beautiful, was always vaguely suspect.") It exists for its own sake, just as the singer sings for his. Birds singing and women laundering clothes are as old as the earth. Neither is a political entity, but their singing is all the articulation of inward freedom Smith has aside from the endless monologue in his head. After a lifetime of deprivation and drudgery, the old prole woman with no cause for carolling but some deathless spirit of life appears to Smith with her own style of beauty. She has "strong arms, a warm heart, and a fertile belly." As long as she sings the Party is threatened by something it cannot control, and Smith feels he can share in the future for which her song convinces him there is "some blessed Hope" if he can keep alive "the secret doctrine that two plus two make four" as she keeps alive elemental feeling.

The snatches of joy with Julia, of freedom from telescreens, and of relaxation in the trust that there is a secret brotherhood which works with him to extend the area of sanity enable Smith to focus his personal memories. He remembers his mother, who, without being unusual or particularly intelligent, had had "a kind of nobility, a kind of purity, simply because the standards that she obeyed were private ones. Her feelings were her own, and could not be altered from outside. It would not have occurred to her that an action which is ineffectual thereby becomes meaningless. If you loved someone, you loved him, and when you had nothing else to give, you still gave him love."

His memory is not altogether free from pain, however, as he finally dredges from the dark bottom of his guilt the particular futile but significant gesture of hers which has haunted him ever since, in the flicks, he watched a refugee mother shielding her child from a rain of bullets with her own vulnerable body. He has to remember that as a child, with sheer predatory ferocity, he betrayed the only two human beings whom he had any right to expect would love him without reason—betrayed them once they had nothing to give him but love. As a child, he was nothing but a stomach, and the power of love was not strong enough to make him share what the power of the Party now compels him to share: a limited amount of chocolate. While rendering you as powerless over the material world as a child is, the Party persuaded you that "mere impulses, mere feelings, were of no account. . . . When once you were in the grip of the Party, what you felt or did not feel, what you did or refrained from doing, made literally no difference. Whatever happened you vanished, and neither you nor your actions were ever heard of again. You were lifted clean out of the stream of history." [13]

Perhaps as terrible as the threat of oblivion is the thought that, for all the Party's efforts to eradicate them, "mere impulses"—being the things they are, not altogether conditioned reflexes but motions which inhere, as God's attributes, in men—are stronger than anyone's power to control them. After all, Syme, Ampleforth, and Parsons come to the same fate as the conscious rebel Winston Smith. Furthermore, when one of the prisoners in the Ministry of Love impulsively throws a crust of bread to a man who, before everyone's eyes, is dying of starvation, it makes "literally no difference," except to increase the pain of the other prisoners and to insure the torments of the man who injudiciously yielded to impulse. The bread lies on the floor as fatally condemning as Julia's "I Love You" lies in the palm of Smith's hand. In an age that worships not the God of Love, nor even the relatively innocuous God of Money, but pure power, Orwell saw the chilling possibility that evanescent private virtues—Love, Mercy, Pity, Peace (which vanish in the grip of ideologies laying claim to them as unalterable laws)—may cease to have meaning if they always prove futile.

Orwell feared not only the disappearance of these virtues in totalitarian systems which had no use for them and much to fear from them. In each of his novels there runs a strong apprehension that youth, beauty, love, spontaneity, and joy must yield to the force which, barely obstructed in its career, strove always for domination over the weak. The golden country, the paradise of those who do not want to smash faces, is a region not of this world. It is a place

> Where the youth, pined away with desire
> And the pale Virgin shrouded in snow
> Arise from their graves, and aspire
> Where my Sun-flower wishes to go.
>
> —William Blake, "Ah Sunflower! Weary of Time"

In time spent counting the steps of the Sun, the young grow old, their desires cloud, they become "weary of time" and dim with regrets. The green, as it empties and darkens at nightfall, echoes with the lost joys of childhood: "Such, such were the joys. . . ." The phrase has a dying fall, a quality of nostalgia for the fleeting instants when life on this earth did not seem wholly meaningless and dreadful. The pining youths and cold virgins seek but seldom find that "sweet golden clime" their hearts desire.

Gordon Comstock and Rosemary, like Winston Smith and Julia, meet originally in the corridors of a large impersonal building. They are fellow employees in different departments of an advertising firm the principles of which Comstock despises and Rosemary is indifferent to. Like Julia, Rosemary is dark and attractive "but rather intimidating." As her acquaintance with Comstock ripens, it is beset with difficulties put in the way by Comstock's one-man revolt against the shameless cohabitation of Greed and Respectability. Finally, desperate without Rosemary and determined to attack her sexual reticence as a hateful symptom of bourgeois hypocrisy, Comstock cadges money for a day in the country with her, largely because it is the cheapest kind of day and promises him a chance to have his will with a woman.

> This woman business! What a bore it is! What a pity we can't cut it right out, or at least be like the animals—minutes of ferocious lust and months of icy chastity. . . . Lucky pheasant! How different from the lord of creation, always on the hop between his memory and his conscience! [14]

Comstock has extracted from Rosemary her tacit consent to be his when they "get an opportunity." They start off together "extravagantly happy" and full of "absurd enthusiasm" over everything they see. The fall leaves with the sun on them "really are like gold." But as they grow hungry and footsore the clouds gather, and the countryside which should be filled with cozy—and cheap—pubs yields only a bleak resort hotel where they are fleeced for bad food and service. Their meal there is relieved of horror only briefly when they notice two swans on the river that seem to have followed them. The sun bursts splendidly forth again and, under the warmth generated by the wine he can't afford, Comstock imagines their destiny: "some hidden place in the warm, windless air." Sitting together with their knees locked under the table, they feel a "deep intimacy" and become oblivious of the insolent waiter. "But presently the sun went in, the room grew grey again," and the young lovers leave, their "warm intimacy" dispelled: "Everything seemed different now that they were outisde." Their blood has cooled, and Comstock, sensing Rosemary's nervousness, wishes only that the deed were done, not that it were yet to do. They come to a small copse of naked trees and enter it under barbed wire. They find a spot where the grass is fine and mossy. When they lie down, Rosemary is frightened and Comstock dismayed to find "how little, at this moment, he really wanted her." This perverse state of affairs is dispelled in its turn by the sun's emerging from the clouds and gilding what is ugly. Rosemary's nakedness is startlingly beautiful, and, despite the disheartening clink of the pennies in his trousers, Comstock is ready to redeem the promise her body has made. But the money-god wins this round, as Rosemary realizes Comstock has taken no precautions not to make a baby. Their day ends with Comstock's bitter harangue against respectability and a hopeless wail from Rosemary: "What am I to do?" The sun disappears, the air grows "perceptibily colder," and the scene—a naked virgin and a fully-clad lover whose moment of "ferocious lust" passes unconsummated—strikes even the would-be deflowerer as ludicrous.

The rapport between Comstock and Rosemary is as elusive and subject to externals as the moments between Flory and Elizabeth which promise Flory that Elizabeth's response matches his. These two have met under circumstances that seem an answer to Flory's lonely prayer. He has performed as her heroic defender against a harmless water buffalo, and with genuine fright and gratitude Elizabeth clings to his arm. The sun is warm, her short hair is "yellow," and her "soft youthful body" breathes warmth against his. As they walk together in this first acquaintance, the sun grows stronger; a wave of scent from the wild fruit and flowers caresses them. A pigeon startles into flight, and they stop, "with one consent, to look at the flowers." Both are shot through with a "pang of unreasonable happiness."

Only once after that is any delicious rapport established between them. When Flory places the limp, warm body of the bird she has shot into Elizabeth's hands, she is ravished. In an ecstasy quite alien to her nature (but inspired, of course, by her "ferocious lust" to destroy), she kisses and hugs the dead bird and then, relinquishing it, becomes "conscious of an extraordinary desire to fling her arms around Flory's neck and kiss him." After Flory proves his markmanship by bagging the leopard, the two of them walk together, Elizabeth's shoulder "almost touching Flory's," their faces illuminated by a "yellow, gentle beam" from the setting sun. Such, such are the only joys of these two.

George Bowling tells the story of Elsie only because Elsie was "part of the picture . . . 'before the war.' Before the war it was always summer"—the dace swimming lazy under the willows and nothing to do but fish and make love. When Bowling met Elsie she was "curiously soft" and endowed with a remarkable pale blond beauty, "deeply feminine, very gentle, very submissive" and sexually generous. Because of Elsie, Bowling as a young man missed his chance of going to look again at his secret pool before it vanished for good. Her boldness in sexual initiative resembles that of Rosemary when, finally, in defiance of consequences she comes to Comstock's room and takes him. Both women are prototypes for

Julia, who in a single gesture unzips the Party uniform and stands before Smith in the warm air, naked and unstinting.

But before Bowling leaves Binfield in his middle-aged odyssey, he spends a disillusioning interval which once and for all dispels his memories of "July nights under the chestnut tree" with Elsie. As he walks behind her thickened body, he tries to remember her red lips, her "milky-white skin" and "dull-gold hair." The woman he walks behind is not simply middle-aged; she is "a kind of soft, lumpy cylinder, like a bag of meal." She has undergone a transformation physically so complete as to render her sexually repellent. Her speech has suffered a comparable degeneracy, and her memory—"she'd simply forgotten my existence," Bowling reports.

The transformation of Julia, if one considers how much less time has probably elapsed, is even more shocking. It is "vilely cold" when she and Smith meet in the park. Two and two now make five, and Smith wonders why he ever bothered to rebel. The only thing that might conceivably stir him from his gin-induced euphoria is the body of the slender dark-haired girl who lay in the dust of the bell-tower with him as the sun set on their afternoon of lovemaking. But Smith's flesh now freezes at the very thought of making love. Julia is unresponsive and sallow; "her waist had grown thicker and, in a surprising way, had stiffened." The "rigidity and awkwardness" of her body are like a corpse's, and it occurs to Smith that even the "texture of her skin" would have changed. The contrast between the thing she was and the thing she has become proves to Smith the difference between being alive and being dead which, rapt by political insights, he once denied, provoking Julia at the time to press vigorously against him and exclaim: "Oh, rubbish! Which would you sooner sleep with, me or a skeleton? Don't you enjoy being alive? Don't you like feeling: This is me, this is my hand, this is my leg, I'm real, I'm solid, I'm alive! Don't you like *this*?" [15]—that is, sex?

In the end, this same but altered Julia reminds one of nothing so much as Smith's wife, Katharine, who, when she was performing her "duty to the Party," seemed to "be pushing him from her with all her strength" even as she grappled him to her.

The denouement of *1984* is especially ruthless because the moments Smith and Julia spend in the golden country are as nearly perfect as Orwell could ever allow the tentative rapture of the senses to be. Like Bowling, when he gets to the country Smith has an irresistible urge to pick flowers. In the broad May sunshine he at first feels "dirty" and "etiolated" and is slow to act once Julia has led him to a thin wood of ash trees. Then suddenly her body is strained against his, the mass of her dark hair against his face. Even then, though Julia is "utterly unresisting," Smith has no physical desire, and Julia stops him to talk and adjust to the miracle of being alone with a woman who has no motive except love for making love. They listen to the thrush pouring its music into the mild air. "It was as though it were a kind of liquid stuff that poured all over him and got mixed up with the sunlight that filtered through the leaves. He stopped thinking and merely felt."

Then, with a magnificence that seems to annihilate a "whole civilization," Julia flings aside her uniform and Smith, not yet looking at her body, kneels before her. After their union, they sleep; and, watching Julia's "young, strong body" still "helpless in sleep" while he is awake, Smith is suffused with a "pitying, protective feeling. But the mindless tenderness that he had felt under the hazel tree, while the thrush was singing, had not quite come back." Already the purity of that intense joy fades, and Smith coolly analyzes its ulterior effect: "Their embrace had been a battle, the climax a victory."

The land in which this victory is achieved is the landscape Smith has sometimes seen in dreams. Without hesitation he denominates it the Golden Country.

> He knew it by sight. An old, close-bitten pasture, with a footpath wandering across it and a molehill here and there. In the ragged hedge on the opposite side the boughs of the elm trees swayed just perceptibly in the breeze, and their

> leaves stirred faintly in dense masses like women's hair. Surely somewhere near by, but out of sight, there must be a stream with green pools where dace were swimming.[16]

It is a landscape of George Bowling's boyhood, it is almost identical with that which Comstock and Rosemary survey on their afternoon in the country, and it returns once more to Smith in the interval of recovery he is permitted between his stage of "understanding" and the final stage of "acceptance." In this interval, although he has seen the human form divine destroyed, Smith knows that at least he has not betrayed Julia. He sinks into an effortless reverie of the Golden Country, where he strolls with Julia, his mother, and O'Brien. They talk of "peaceful things." He is content merely to be alive and feel health return to his body. Incapable of fresh intellectual effort, he has been rehearsing the truth that sanity, after all, *is* statistical and that GOD IS POWER. But when from the Golden Country Julia suddenly cries out to him, seemingly, for help, the "pitying, protective feeling" returns, and Smith knows his surrender to God has not been complete. His love for Julia, recurring with unbidden intensity, strengthens his almost forgotten resolve: "To die hating them, that was freedom."

Of course, O'Brien is true to his word: "We shall squeeze you empty, and then we shall fill you with ourselves." Ironically, in the place where there is no darkness, a place always imaginatively entangled in Smith's imagination with the sun-flooded Golden Country, Smith sheds his humanity and with it the coil of mortal guilt. In the final chapter of his story, the armies of unalterable law advance, victorious, on the telescreen: Big Brother is omnipotent indeed and Oceania is immortal. Smith's agitation subsides after a dreadful last moment of doubting these truths. For winning the victory over himself, Smith is rewarded with a more perfect love. It is now, truly, unimportant whether he lives or dies, for he lives in a single moment which is the same for all time—his "false memories" vanquished forever. The "final, indispensable, healing change" at last occurs. "O cruel, needless misunderstanding! O stubborn, self-willed exile from the loving breast!" At last nothing can impinge upon his "blissful dream." He is back in the place where the light never fails, "with everything forgiven, his soul white as snow."

Winston Smith has ceased to be human for very human reasons. In Room 101 he has been "firmly perswaded" by his senses that something is so. Sheer physical repugnance has succeeded where pain and O'Brien's psycho-therapy have failed. The past and the future have been subsumed by the eternal present in which the Party makes whatever happens "right." With gin-scented tears bathing his cheeks, Smith approaches Nirvana, a blissful dream of paradise for those who give over the stubborn struggle to see things as they are. In a hideous perversion of traditional eschatological visions, Smith's refuge in the pseudo-religion of Big Brotherhood is distinctly other-worldly. The world of sensory appearances and concrete objects has given way to a world constructed on the assumption that two and two equal whatever the Party says they equal. The only way to be "right" all the time is to accept the inscrutable, omniscient God's determination of all things. "Reality is only in the mind," and the mind is created in the image of its maker.

Precisely because Orwell believed "all real happenings are in the mind," [17] he could imagine the ultimate lunatic dislocation of the divine gift of reason. The subtle affinity Smith feels for O'Brien may be simply a mutual dread of oblivion and a longing for immortality, for some hope that life is not as utterly purposeless, disorderly, and disagreeable as it seems. As the Big Brother assigned to Smith, O'Brien performs the great kindness of helping Smith to lose his mind—and his sensibility. In proportion as the world men live in lacks an objective reality which their senses can approve, they will create realities in the few cubic centimeters of their skull to supplant it. Smith's initial effort to reconstruct history is assisted not only by his memory, which, without verification, he must suspect, but by tangible objects which have the durability to stay in the world as earnests of the world's reality and permanence, as constructs of man's hand, eye, and brain. This world is opposed to simple nature, which may, in a pinch, nurture biological life. The world is the specific domain of significance, the realm not of predictable, statistical items but of unique, inviolable persons who modify the world by their appearance in it.

It is curious that each of Orwell's novels (except for *Animal Farm,* which after all deals with animals and in which the human-like pigs *are* housed as man is housed) presents the biological continuance of the species as something alientated from, defeated by, or carried on in spite of the man-made world, as though the simple, unconscious life-force were in some sinister way jeopardized by the world's purposes and instinctively sought exile in a golden land where men and women could talk of peaceful things and where their intimacy could be both open and sheltered, without shame and yet without surveillance.

Winston Smith tries to recreate a world outside the world he lives in, to ressurect a time when man had not "succeeded in doing his dirt every where," a time Orwell conceived of before the first world war "when England was still prosperous" and unfrightened, a time which reminded him that his age had "not been altogether a bad one to live in." [18]

In a settled period when "civilisation seems to stand on its four legs like an elephant," men have no need to plot utopias in accordance with some ideological, inflexible absolute. The way of God and the way of Man seem to be in harmony, and the moral platitudes of Christian feeling suffice to distinguish good and evil. Without, however, a competence of the good things of life—food, warmth, companionship, privacy, work for the hand and brain, stimuli for the senses—man is liable to dream of Sugarcandy Mountain, to regard life merely as a preparation for something beyond the grave, or to delude himself with some ideology which copes with phenomena by denying their empirical reality. To do the latter, of course, is to ignore the report of the senses altogether and to outlaw common sense.

Orwell could conceive of such lunacy with mordant humor—as one pig's stealing credit for another pig's electrification plans after pissing publicly upon them. The lunatic has always had a firm persuasion that a thing is so, even when it is not; but in his century, for the first time in history, Orwell realized the means were at the disposal of international lunatics to impose their "world-view" totalitarianly.

Certainly Orwell had his own firm persuasions, a kind of prophetic faith like Blake's that there was a right way to be and that an unflinching adherence to this way could snap even the chains forged in an oppressor's fire. But his faith was always disciplined by the abrasive realities: sheer force combining with the psychological torments of relentless propaganda and brainwashing, the tyranny even of hunger, pain, boredom, and disgust, and the overshadowing of ideas by ideologies. The magnitude of these forces frightened him, but the inside of the whale frightened him even more. "Nowadays the present and the future are too terrifying to be escaped from. . . ." [19] Unlike the quietist, he fell into neither extreme, neither "complete unbelief" nor "a degree of belief amounting to mysticism"; but empiricism on the one hand and a dogged faith on the other are the poles between which his thought and feeling ply. Like Blake he trusts that somehow the earth, imprisoned in a dangerous sleep ("Grave the sentence deep"), shall shake itself and convert desert wastes into "a garden mild." [20] At the same time he sees the "echoing green" of childhood joys grow empty and dark, the democratic vistas end in barbed wire, the unborn and the unconscious threatened by an unspeakable peril which in their somnolence they are helpless against.

Upon occasion, like Blake, he admonishes the "princes of fire" to regard all men as equals: "Thy brethren, and not as thy foot or thy hand, unless thou first fearest to hurt them." In *1984* and elsewhere he conceives of humanity as a helpless organism suffering infinite pain because its parts (the leaders the brain, the administration its hands, and the slumbrous masses the body of perpetual, instinctive animal life) do not co-operate in the health of the whole.

Finally, like Blake he sees that the golden lads and lasses must come to dust. Earth might be the right place for love; Orwell did not think there was really a place where it was likely to go better. But in his fiction it does not go well. In

Burmese Days it is the plaything of caste snobbery. In *Keep the Aspidistra Flying* it is almost sabotaged by the almighty dollar. In *A Clergyman's Daughter* it is up against a constitutional squeamishness in Dorothy, who—nice girl as she is—qualifies as a charter member for the Anti-Sex League. In *Coming Up for Air* Bowling's first love is a war casualty, his second an infatuation for all the wrong reasons: the opposites no sooner attract than they repel each other; their relation further deteriorates in the essential insincerity of the world they inhabit.

In *1984* love is, in the last analysis, a political act, a blow struck for freedom, in that one man and one woman assert the dominance of passion—sheer appetite—against the decree that nothing shall be enjoyed. Julia, however, is a hedonist. Smith alone is a political rebel. He alone cares about something more than mere survival, more certainly than momentary personal gratification. What he cares about pre-eminently is the *world,* the specifically human domain in which biological process gains meaning despite the grave to which particular men go.

> For this world of ours, because it existed before us and is meant to outlast our lives in it, simply cannot afford to give primary concern to individual lives and the interests connected with them; as such the public realm stands in the sharpest possible contrast to our private domain, where, in the protection of family and home, everything serves and must serve the security of the life process. It requires courage even to leave the protective security of our four walls and enter the public realm, not because of particular dangers which may lie in wait for us, but because we have arrived in a realm where the concern for life has lost its validity. Courage liberates men from their worry about life for the freedom of the world. Courage is indispensable because in politics not life but the world is at stake.[21]

It is worldlessness which bothers Smith and which bothered Orwell to the extent of imagining a time when even the intimate was no longer a secure retreat. What remained of the "privateness" of human life was really no guarantee of freedom; it was simply the helpless victim of totalitarian systems. For it is impossible for a totalitarian "fiction," as Arendt calls it, to impose itself successfully as long as any alternative way of life remains conceivable, even if it is the limited way of apolitical family men. Totalitarianism must invade and destroy, then, the final refuge: the inside of the whale.

The world totally destroyed by violence is not nearly as horrible to imagination as a planet inhabited eternally by catatonic masses ruled by madmen obsessed with destroying whatever does not conform to their world-view and intolerant of anything which challenges the certainty and perfection of life under the system, whether it is "Ingsoc," "Neo-Bolshevism," or "Death-worship." Orwell knew that controlled insanity has an immense appeal for those unequal to the hard work of living and loving, those unable to face the possibility that human life may never be perfect. Against the ideological soma which would drown the wakeful anguish of the human soul he crusaded with all the passion of a poet who sees the "ages of imagination" in swift retreat. Not only with Blake but with other Englishmen he shared a prophetic vision of Britain founded in a tenderness for her people and their way of life which was *humanly* rather than *racially* proud. Had there been time, such a vision would have moved Hotspur to prophesy. It caused even the youthful classicist Pope to extol the "brave Britons" who "foreign laws despised, / And kept unconquered, and uncivilized." Perhaps it caused the disabled Milton to attempt defiantly to soar, in his cold clime, "above the Aonian mount" and to conceive of the earth itself in the image of England's isle, vulnerable and beautiful, a "pendant world, in bigness as a Star / Of smallest magnitude," beset by "hellish foes anow" but under the egis of a provident God—a "sceptred isle," a "demi-paradise"—"this earth, this realm, this England."

The prophets thus inspired, and Orwell is one of them, have a vision not of national glory or Fatherlands militant but a vision of the world which the world hardly understands—of the earth as a good place where, against all odds, men must foster liberty and justice and a belief in human dignity.

CHAPTER SIX

THE CHOSEN PEOPLE

. . . something, some psychological vitamin, is lacking in modern civilisation, and as a result we are all more or less subject to this lunacy of believing that whole races or nations are mysteriously good or mysteriously evil.

—Orwell, "Anti-Semitism in Britain" in "Such, Such Were the Joys"

The powers of good and evil, once mystically assigned to remote extraterrestrial regions, seem in recent centuries to have taken up permanent abode on the already overcrowded earth and begun, like everyone else, to play politics. They have lost much of their disinterestedness and universality, while retaining their atavistic aspect as forces beyond man's control. Assuming what shape, sex, and title they please, they choose sides where it seems the battle of heaven must ultimately be decided: on earth.

Orwell complains of James Burnham that, for all his preoccupation with the struggle for power, he never wrestled with the question that haunts Winston Smith—and which Orwell, in the last analysis, never answers for him: *why* do people want power? and the question which Orwell formulates with even greater incredulity: "why does the lust for naked power become a major human motive exactly *now,* when the dominion of man over man is ceasing to be necessary?" [1]

Perhaps it is impossible for anyone who has not been drunk with power to understand, let alone explain, the "intoxication of power" and to Orwell's credit that he could not; but, whether the worship of power is the modern form which awe of superior forces takes or whether it must remain, to those who experience its consequences in the terrestrial struggle, as inscrutable as it remains to Orwell, how to prevent the abuse of power is an issue Orwell continually addresses himself to, and the problem repeatedly brings him face to face with the modern form of tyranny: totalitarianism. There are tyrannies and there are tyrannies, and Orwell does not worry about all of them. In a consideration of tyrannies, the "distinction that really matters," he says, "is not between violence and non-violence, but between having and not having the appetite for power." [2]

From the Orwellian analysis of the problem, it appears that the appetite for power is sharpest in those who cannot bear to be wrong, even for the few score years of mortal existence—or perhaps because those few score years seem today to be all the eternity any of us will have. It may be that the "pursuit of truth" compressed into a short span and uncrowned by the promise of revelation after death drives us in the twentieth century upon what Conrad calls "paths of excessive cruelties and excessive devotions."

The disease of the modern world, at any rate, is the worship of power, an adoration of devils as though they were deities, which Orwell designates by the term "nationalism." In his "notes" on this subject Orwell observes that nationalism always uncritically labels large groups of people good or bad and finds itself—it goes without saying—among the right people. Nationalism is "inescapable from the desire for power," power not for oneself but for the group in which a man "has chosen to sink his own individuality." The identifying symptom of this modern disease is "power-hunger tempered by self-deception." The patient is capable, Orwell says, "of the most flagrant dishonesty" and, convinced of the transcendent nature of his devotion, he is "unshakeably certain of being in the right." [3] Especially, Orwell says, if you embrace "a creed which appears to be free from the ordinary dirtiness of politics," one from which you stand to derive no tangible profit, you are convinced of your moral superiority. "And the more you are in the right, the more natural that everyone else should be bullied into thinking likewise." [4]

Of paramount importance to the nationalist is the serene conviction of infallibility: "the object of his feelings is changeable, and may be imaginary," whether that object is the Fatherland, the New Jerusalem, Big Brotherhood, psychic regeneration through health foods, anti-vivisectionism or anti-semitism. If some sort of "dislocation has taken place," an idol must be found to replace the idols that have fallen, and the past as well as the present must be brought into line with the adopted vision. The English leftist, the "nationalist" closest for discomfort to Orwell, obliged to manifest his emancipation from traditional faiths in God and country, looks abroad for idols which can be "worshipped with a good conscience." This "transferred nationalism," Orwell says, "like the use of scapegoats, is a way of attaining salvation without altering one's conduct." [5] It is in the name of such "transferred nationalism" that the most "slavish and boastful rubbish" gets written and the grossest distortions of reality get into history.

> The primary aim of propaganda is, of course, to influence contemporary opinion, but those who rewrite history do probably believe with part of their minds that they are actually thrusting facts into the past. . . . that their own version *was* what happened in the sight of God, and that one is justified in re-arranging the records accordingly.

Such self-deceivers, of course, "are not far from schizophrenia, living quite happily amid dreams of power and conquest which have no connection with the physical world." [6] Happiness, as Jonathan Swift says, is the "perpetual possession of being well-deceiv'd"—a sort of madness he castigated two centuries before Orwell.

Not everyone is infected with the disease—at least not all the time. But the pure nationalist is "barely sane"; he has no "neutral areas in his mind and no interest in anything except the struggle for power." Even ordinarily fair-minded persons, when their sore spot is touched, become vicious partisans,

Orwell says, "anxious only to 'score'" over their adversaries and unscrupulous in the means to this end. "One prod to the nerve of nationalism, and the intellectual decencies can vanish, the past can be altered, and the plainest facts . . . denied." [7] The moral sense, along with the "sense of reality," becomes "unhinged." As long as "our side" commits them, there are absolutely no crimes "that cannot be condoned." In saner moments one may know such crimes are unconscionable in any cause, but one nevertheless *feels* they are right in The Cause. "Loyalty is involved," Orwell says, "so pity ceases to function." [8]

It might as well be some "vitamin" deficiency that makes the best of us susceptible to virulent types of nationalism, but Orwell contends that the disease can be fought. There is no successful quarantine, however. Escapism is simply a subspecies of nationalism. But, if side-taking is inescapable, "some causes are objectively better than others, even if they are advanced by equally bad means" and presumably, unless sanity today is impossible, one can support a cause for objectively sound reasons. One's subrational feelings are, of course, "inescapable, and are perhaps even necessary to political action," but they should be able to coexist "with an acceptance of reality." As a specific against lunacy, Orwell prescribes "moral effort." [9]

Admittedly, great effort is required to make choices in a political sphere, where good and bad are far from being absolute. But for Orwell totalitarianism—the "nationalism" which contains all others in itself and prescribes a view of reality fixed in every detail, is the "radical evil" (as Hannah Arendt calls it) of the twentieth century thus far—for the particular reason, perhaps, that just when man has arrived at a point in his history when dominion over his fellow men is no longer necessary he has discovered the key to total power. Being omnipotent, he can stand no bar to omniscience. Like a madman, he abandons the slow miracles of thought and blinds himself with excess of light. The old-fashioned perfectionist might have been content to do away with himself rather than live in a world which would not comply with his vision. The modern perfectionist, however, has the means to impose his vision upon everyone else, or simply, like the Nazis, to do away once and for all with the "bad" which opposes the "good."

The disease of nationalism has the insidious habit of creeping up on those who, watching the progress of the disease in others, consider themselves perfectly sound. The timorous who fear contagion argue that in fighting the disease we will come down with it. Although in *1984* Smith runs this very risk, Orwell contemptuously counters the argument that "if we fight against the Nazis we shall 'go Nazi' ourselves." Those who so argue "might almost equally well say that if we fight against Negroes we shall turn black." [10] The fatalism of such an argument bears the same simplistic tendency of all nationalisms: war is bad; therefore capitulation is good. The English intelligentsia of the Left, during the second world war, Orwell charges, suffered a form of the disease adapted to their constitutional impatience with half-truths and half-measures. "Their morale was worse because their imaginations were stronger" than most men's; and, like Conrad's Jim faced with the impossibility of rescuing eight-hundred helpless pilgrims before the *Patna* should sink under him, they stood aloof from the ludicrous and undignified efforts of the common people to save at least their own skins. "The quickest way of ending a war is to lose it, and if one finds the prospect of a long war intolerable, it is natural to disbelieve in the possibility of victory." [11]

The intellectual's predictions of doom, like James Burnham's, Orwell finds fallacious for the simple reason that they predict *"a continuation of the thing that is happening*. Now the tendency to do this is not simply a bad habit, like inaccuracy or exaggeration, which one can correct by taking thought. It is a major mental disease, and its roots lie partly in cowardice and partly in the worship of power, which is not fully separable from cowardice." [12] It pained Orwell that the very "genuinely progressive impulses" which should make men adamantly opposed to enemies of human freedom could mix subtly with an unconscious "admiration for power and cruelty"—an admiration implicit in the fatalistic conviction that whoever is "winning at the moment" is "invincible." [13]

This fatalism in James Burnham Orwell relates to the simplistic extremism in the American world-view. He deplores the American tough realism (whether imperialist or isolationist) as a form of "wish-thinking." The Americans, he complains, could indulge their admiration of Nazi brutality because the Atlantic "is wider than the Channel," and because it matters little to the American whether Communism or Fascism wins out. Either way, his country will "survive as a great power." The American of Orwell's imagination is little better than the Communist caricature of the capitalist exploiter who drinks the blood of the poor to the musical accompaniment of money gathering interest: Orwell coolly asserts that "most Americans" would be relieved to see the world resolve itself into "two or three monster states" devoted exclusively to economic villainies and untroubled by ideological concerns. For Americans "admire size for its own sake" and believe that "success constitutes justification." Orwell grudgingly admits America has been "forced" to fight Germany and will probably be forced, against her preferences, to ally herself with Britain against Russia. It may have been Orwell's preternatural tenderness for the "genius of the English people" that made American Anglophobia a sore spot with him and made him declare, defensively, that Americans "would prefer either Russia or Germany to Britain and, as between Russia and Germany, . . . whichever seemed stronger at the moment." [14]

But with or without America's support, Orwell contended during the war and after it that the time for democratic socialism had arrived. Neither "human nature" nor "inexorable laws" made it impossible. The argument that, simply "because a society of free and equal human beings has never existed, it can never exist" seemed to Orwell another instance of predicting the future as a continuation of what is happening. "The huge, invincible, everlasting slave empire . . . will not be established or, if established, will not endure, because slavery is no longer a stable basis for human society." [15] Why,

Orwell does not explain. His own prediction here has the noble temerity of a leap into faith. Surely in *1984* he conceives of precisely the invincible monster states which he accuses Burnham of "dreaming" of. But if, unlike Swift, he possessed "ordinary wisdom," Orwell, like Swift, possessed a "terrible intensity of vision, capable of picking out a single hidden truth and then magnifying it and distorting it." [16] With his ordinary, workaday wisdom, Orwell believed sincerely enough that even if you had to resort to "force and cunning" to achieve revolutionary goals and thus "pervert your original aims" (of combining power with righteousness), an Everlasting Yea was better than an Everlasting No: "All revolutions are failures, but they are not all the same failure." [17]

One may infer that the Spanish revolution, for example, was a better failure than the Russian revolution precisely because it failed before the righteousness which inspired it had been exhausted in the exercise of power. The idea of equality and justice survived in the minds of those who fought for it or witnessed its martyrdoms. So Orwell felt that if England were to awaken to her true genius, to a recognition of her role as the custodian and defender of freedom, even her defeat would not be ultimate; for "the struggle would continue, the *idea* would survive." There was a difference between "going down fighting, and surrendering without a fight." The latter, as even Hitler knew, "destroys the soul of a nation." [18]

But it was not enough for Orwell that Britain should defeat Nazism and simply defend the status quo at home. "Nothing ever stands still," he declared in 1941. "We must add to our heritage or lose it, . . . grow greater or grow less, . . . go forward or backward. I believe in England, and I believe that we shall go forward." [19] And so he urges the common people, who have more to lose than their chains in the confrontation of democracy and totalitarianism, to define their war aims. To the Socialists he says, "We have got to make our words take physical shape or perish." The day was past that one could be a Socialist *and* have a good time. The moment demanded, if not the surrender of life, the sacrifice of "leisure, comfort, economic liberty, social prestige"—Socialist goals temporarily expendable in the struggle against tyranny. But war, Orwell declares, "is the greatest of all agents of change" in that it makes the individual aware "that he is *not* altogether an individual," not free, for instance, to decline service to his country on the basis of some idiosyncratic truth. It is only when men are aware that they are not islands unto themselves that they "will die on the field of battle." [20] Before they can live as individuals the world has to be saved—since the world is *at stake*—and the positive salvation of the world is the "growth of democratic consciousness" which Orwell invariably designates as the basic assumption of socialism.

If war is to be an agent of change, Orwell says it must be conceived as a "struggle between the groping and the unteachable, between the young and the old, between the living and the dead" not only abroad but at home.[21] The genuine revolutionary, in Orwell's view, is never an "internationalist"; he is always a patriot. And patriotism, unlike conservatism, is a "devotion to something that is always changing and yet is felt to be mystically the same. It is the bridge between the future and the past." [22] It envisions not the defense of the status quo but an appropriate response to the needs of a growing organism, and Britain's needs as Orwell believed the Socialist should formulate them are specific political goals which would make winning the war a tangible good for the common people: the limitation of incomes, the democratization of education, the granting of equal partnership to India (including her option to "secede" from it), the establishment of a council of "coloured peoples" for the working out of their destinies in the framework of the free world, and a formal alliance with the victims of the fascist powers.

As Orwell saw it, only a Socialist government could accomplish these aims without hypocrisy. English socialism, he says, will continue

> the tradition of compromise and the belief in a law that is above the State. It will shoot traitors, but . . . give them a solemn trial beforehand and occasionally . . . acquit them. It will crush any open revolt promptly and cruelly, but it

> will interfere very little with the spoken and written word. Political parties . . . will still exist, revolutionary sects will still be publishing their newspapers and making as little impression as ever. It will disestablish the Church, but will not persecute religion. It will retain a vague reverence for the Christian moral code. . . . It will show a power of assimilating the past which will shock foreign observers and sometimes make them doubt whether any revolution has happened.[23]

Perhaps in this war-time prediction Orwell showed that he understood so well the "English genius" for making revolutions without fuss that it was safe to project the past and present into the future and depend on a continuation of what had been happening in England: the accommodation, sometimes clumsy, usually belated, but nevertheless the accommodation, of her various unequal family members with some formal semblance of equality and justice, so that twenty years later observers dispute whether or not a revolution has taken place.

Despite Orwell's opposition of patriotism to internationalism, some of his loyalties can be comprehended only by an extension of the terms he used. If patriotism is the defense of a particular cherished way of life in the faith that it is the best way on earth, with no concomitant impulse to bully other people into adopting it, if it is a tyranny of the heart, mind, and senses that exacts loyalty to the death in its defense, requiring sometimes even violence and cruelty but never the appetite for power, then surely the "democratic consciousness" has outgrown strictly national boundaries and is international enough to have drawn the lines of struggle across the Atlantic and Pacific, to say nothing of channels, canals, and archipelagos. In so far as Orwell himself confessed that Britain's potential allies were not the Europeans but the Americans and the "coloured peoples," he himself roughly drew a sphere of influence in which this democratic consciousness was most likely to thrive, from well-established roots or in virgin soil. Whether or not one is willing to predict a continuation on the basis of what is happening (one's imagination guided as it is by the division of the world in *1984* and influenced by the recent rift between the "Eurasian" and "Eastasian" versions of communism), one is tempted to regard Orwell's own version of the struggle between good and evil as a tacit homage to "Oceania," the area of what remains of the self-consciously "free world" and the as yet uncommitted emergent nations of the African continent.

Orwell's dream for the world easily escaped the territorial limits of the British Commonwealth; clearly he did not regard England as an island unto herself. "Two incompatible visions of life," Orwell asserts, "are fighting one another." Totalitarianism and democracy "cannot even, for any length of time, live side by side."

> So long as democracy exists, even in its very imperfect English form, totalitarianism is in deadly danger. The whole English-speaking world is haunted by the idea of human equality, and though it would be simply a lie to say that either we or the Americans have ever acted up to our professions, still, the *idea* is there, and it is capable of one day becoming a reality. From the English-speaking culture, if it does not perish, a society of free and equal human beings will ultimately arise.[24]

Totalitarianism is intent not so much upon overcoming its enemies in war as in destroying what Orwell calls the "'Judaeo-Christian' idea of equality" for blacks, for whites, for Jews, for maiden aunts and bankers, for Colonel Blimps and ineffectual radicals alike. Mrs. Parsons' intellectual prowess may not hold a candle to O'Brien's, but the idea of equality entitles her to have her drain-pipe cleared and her children, forcibly if necessary, kept from terrorizing their father. "With all its sloth, hypocrisy and injustice," Orwell notes, the "English-speaking civilization" was the "only large obstacle in Hitler's path." It was "a living contradiction of all the 'infallible' dogmas of Fascism."[25] If not by the grace of God, then by virtue of tradition, history, and geography, the English-speaking peoples were the elected guardians of freedom. They were the Chosen People in an historic struggle but "good" only in so far as they opposed the "radical evil" of their age.

Whatever else may be true of democracy and totalitarianism, Orwell is sure of one thing: they are not the same and would not be even if democracy failed to evolve "beyond its present stage. The whole conception of the militarized continental state, with its secret police, its censored literature and its conscript labour, is utterly different from that of the loose maritime democracy, with its slums and unemployment, its strikes and party politics." The difference in the tyrannies proper to each is the difference "between cruelty and inefficiency, between lying and self-deception, between the S.S.-man and the rent-collector." One chooses between them on the basis not solely of what they are but of "what they are capable of becoming." And this choice will depend upon "where one's real sympathies will lie when the pinch comes." [26]

One's sympathies quite likely are determined at a subrational level and have to do with one's conception of life itself, with whether one regards it as worth living or as superfluous, not in the philosophical abstract but in one's "inner self." For all he found wrong with life, Orwell remained far from cynical about it. He was as far from dreaming utopias, of course, as he was from approving nihilism. He was, at most, a meliorist, suspicious even of his own reasonable formulas for improving the human condition and politically committed not so much to pushing the world in a direction he wanted it to go as to defending the shrinking area of freedom, justice, and decency in the world. He was an international "patriot" of democracy, so to speak, who felt the world was the only home he had. It was not a question, in his time, of realizing the dream of a perfect society in which there would be "no slavery, no hunger, no injustice, no floggings, no executions." [27] It was a question of preserving the human essence against frightening forces which conspired against it —debasing language, rendering work an intolerable tedium, trusting to miracles instead of to persistence and effort, forcibly replacing variety and free choice by uniformity and predictability. He regarded the desire to establish paradise on earth as a limited and basically hedonistic desire, universal among men yet incompatible with their best interests: "Men can only be happy when they do not assume that the object of life is happiness." Whether or not perfection was desirable was, for Orwell, beside the point; perhaps, he conjectures, it just "isn't possible. Perhaps some degree of suffering is ineradicable from human life, perhaps the choice before man is always a choice of evils, perhaps even the aim of Socialism is not to make the world perfect but to make it better." [28]

If one bothers—as Orwell bothered—with history at all, it is as he said "in order to find modern meanings there," [29] to take a sustained look at the worst which has happened in order to discern alternatives. Both *Animal Farm* and *1984* take a sustained look at the worst without flinching. The fictional mode of each determines that its created semblance should be that of history: what has happened. Rightly speaking, neither is prediction; perhaps, as George Woodcock suggests, at least about *1984*,[30] both may be seen as satires in Swiftian vein, and as relentless as *Gulliver's Travels* in tracking down man's besetting evil. The evil, of course, however it is personified in isms and anti-isms, lies in man. It may be that for Orwell, as for Swift, the ultimate evil is pride: man's thinking too much of himself. Gulliver ends in a "lunatic dislocation" of reason which persuades him that, after a sojourn with the "Perfection of Nature," he is superior to his species. He is madly impatient with human nature, its constitutional tardiness in conforming to the Ideal; but unlike O'Brien Gulliver lacks the means to create human nature or to impose upon it forcibly.

Gulliver is not, as recent criticism makes him out to be, a victim either of Swift's madness or of rationality. He is the pawn of a deliberate satiric purpose, the ultimate illustration of the pride of the strutting animal which Swift shows to be ineradicable. If he who has had the educational advantages of consorting with creatures governed altogether by reason proves incapable of reason in the end, what hope is there for the rest of mankind? Swift's final satiric thrust is at his hero, the relatively good Gulliver, just as Orwell's final thrust is at his hero Smith. Both heroes are expended to make a point.

But Gulliver is defeated by something inherent in his nature, the pride which convinces him that by whinnying and imitating the gait of his masters he has arrived at their wisdom and self-government. He forgets that he has been evicted from Utopia precisely because, although *capable* of reason, he can never be trusted not to misuse his reason to justify wickedness and folly. The Houyhnhnms are too rational to believe that even this relatively cleanly Yahoo is constitutionally capable of being altogether governed by reason. Gulliver merely proves they are right: he unreasonably expects his fellow Yahoos to reform overnight; he arrogates omniscience to himself and in a rage of pride secludes himself from his kind and damns the human race. The point is not that he is wrong about the human race but that he is wrong in thinking himself free of its besetting evil—and it matters not at all that we find Gulliver more attractive than his masters. Our preference, Swift would say, simply proves the irrational pride we take in our folly.

Winston Smith, on the other hand, is up against an insane arrogance, a lunatic more intelligent than he is, who cannot be reached by rational argument, a lunatic, furthermore, omnipotent in an arsenal of mechanical and psychological devices against which the most heroic steadfastness is unavailing. The weight of Orwell's satire falls, it is true, on the presumption of man to be infallible, but it falls on men who are the enemies of man. He leaves man the means to correct or at least curb the direst effects of the evil that lies in himself.

Significantly, Orwell charges Swift with being unable to imagine that "ordinary life on the solid earth, and not some rationalized, deodorized version of it" could through human effort "be made worth living." The question of whether or not it could be, Orwell contends, is the question upon which "all serious political controversy really turns." He sees in Swift's rational utopia "the totalitarian tendency which is explicit in the anarchist or pacifist vision of society."

> In a society in which there is no law, and in theory no compulsion, the only arbiter of behavior is public opinion. But

> public opinion, because of the tremendous urge to conformity in gregarious animals, is less tolerant than any system of law. When human beings are governed by "thou shalt not," the individual can practice a certain amount of eccentricity: when they are supposedly governed by "love" or "reason," he is under continuous pressure to . . . behave and think in exactly the same way as everyone else.[31]

Conformity among the Houyhnhnms, Orwell goes on, has reached the stage every totalitarian organization aspires to. Because there is no dissidence, there is no need for force. (The original Communist dream promised the withering away of the state.) One is exhorted rather than compelled. Truth is a thing so immediately apparent to rational creatures that there can be no difference of opinion. "Swift approves of this kind of thing because among his many gifts neither curiosity nor good-nature was included. Disagreement would always seem to him sheer perversity." [32] Orwell, though, does not approve of this kind of thing at all, finding "totalitarian" unanimity just as oppressive as most readers of *Gulliver's Travels* find it and complaining that such a society lacks both "freedom" and "development." By implication, then, once "nature" has been perfected, *life* is superfluous.

Orwell classifies Swift with those who do not "enjoy even the small amount of happiness that falls to most human beings and, from obvious motives, are not likely to admit that earthly life is capable of much improvement. Their incuriosity, and hence their intolerance, spring from the same root." [33] Swift's pessimism is even less acceptable to Orwell for lacking a vision of a life-to-come, better in all ways than the life-that-is. He suspects that Swift, Dean of St. Patrick's notwithstanding, believed in an after-life no more than George Orwell and so created his paradise fictionally on earth, simply eliminating from it what he disapproved of: "lies, folly, change, enthusiasm, pleasure, love, and dirt." The inhabitants of this paradise are unattractive, Orwell says, because they are exempt from "love, friendship, curiosity, fear, sorrow, and . . . except in their feelings toward the Yahoos, who occupy rather the same place in their community as the Jews in Nazi Germany [and with far greater reason, one should add!]—anger and hatred." [34]

Orwell does not stop to balance his analysis with the observation that, dull as the horses are, they are not nearly as unattractive as the Yahoos and that, in a pinch, one would unhesitatingly choose their clean and mannerly company to that of the least educable of beasts. But Orwell's point about Swift's utopia is a political one: the Reason which governs the Houyhnhnms is "really a desire for death." If, unlike the priests of power in *1984,* the Houyhnhnms have no more appetite for power than they have for sex, they are, like Orwell's ruling saints, careless whether they live or die. And if it does not matter, why do they live at all?

In justice to Swift (who, like all satirists, was more successful in blasting what exists than in constructing what should be) his horses *do* take the highest kind of pleasure in their lives: a rational pleasure, which spares them the degradation of indulgence and the worst excesses of self-deception. Surely Orwell was temperamentally no more of an enthusiast than Swift. But he complains that, instead of devising the vision of a fuller life, Swift "advocates a simple refusal of life," a thwarting of instincts.

> The Houyhnhnms, creatures without a history, continue for generation after generation to live prudently, maintaining their population at exactly the same level, avoiding all passion, suffering from no diseases, meeting death indifferently, training up their young in the same principles—and all for what? In order that the same process may continue indefinitely.

Of course, in a settled period of civilization, that is exactly what *people* do: continue life, with whatever un-utopian harassments, in order that the same process may continue indefinitely. Paradoxically, it was Orwell's good fortune to live in a thoroughly unsettled period, in which man's stature could be gauged by the formidable size of his foes and in which the simplest pleasures seemed all but unattainable. If life were not a preparation for something beyond the grave, its significance had to emerge in effort, in challenges met, in evil overcome. Life was worth living only if it were difficult to live, and Swift's utopia confronts Orwell's reforming zeal with nothing to work upon. "The notions that life here and now is worth living, or that it could be made worth living, or that it must be sacrificed for some future good, are all absent." [35]

Orwell can see no constructive suggestion which this utopia makes, by analogy, to man. It is simply, he says, an excuse for an "attack on humanity" which robs man of dignity and hope. He accuses Swift of the kind of envy a ghost might have for the living, the envy of a man "who knows he cannot be happy for the others who—so he fears—may be a little happier than himself. The political expression of such an outlook must be either reactionary or nihilistic, because the person who holds it will want to prevent society from developing in some direction in which his pessimism may be cheated. One can do this either by blowing everything to pieces, or by averting social change." [36] Or by making modest proposals and pamphleteering against Wood's currency?

The temperamental similarity of Orwell and Swift in both their political and their fictional "expressions" may have caused Orwell to see the pitfalls yawning before him. If anything, the "expression" of the two men shows that Orwell was more frequently governed by reason, Swift more often by tempestuous emotions. But Orwell sensed that Swift was, indeed, what Swift called himself: a misanthrope; and a devotee of democratic socialism could not afford the luxury of such cynicism.

What Orwell had in common with Swift is, in a way, fundamental: a yearning for justice—not just the name for the thing; for an order which permits lives to be led without terror or privation; a feeling that every creature has an innate title to share in the abundance of the earth but not to grab more than his share; an abhorrence of baseness and filth; and above all a desire to push the world in a particular direction. The two part company, however, at a crucial political point which has nothing to do with the superficial fact that Swift was a Tory and Orwell a democrat. Swift, after all, began as a

Whig, and, as Orwell observes, his personal failure to gain preferment may account for his turning not only his political coat but, seemingly, his back on the possibility of human progress. Orwell at least works with a feeling he has that Swift, however passionately moved to political expression by what was wrong with the world, despaired of improving it. The failure of men to solve all the problems capable of solution drove him to the pessimistic conclusion that men fail to solve *any* problems, and what was happening became the basis for predicting what would always happen. The difference between the pessimist and the meliorist is analogous to the difference between an absolutist and a relativist, between a perfectionist and a humanist, between a saint and an "ordinary human being." The difference, Orwell insists, is not of degree but of kind. The saint does not work to improve earthly life but to "bring it to an end and put something different in its place." The humanist, in contrast, believes "that the struggle must continue and that death is the price of life." [37] The "religious and the humanist attitudes toward life" —like the totalitarian and the democratic—are simply, despite seeming truces, irreconcilable: "one must choose between this world and the next," whether the "next" is an after-life or a visionary utopia of the future in which whatever one dislikes is eliminated.

Orwell is confident that "normal human beings" are in the majority and that they do not want the "Kingdom of Heaven": they want "life on earth to continue." They manifest this choice "when they continue working, breeding, and dying instead of crippling their faculties in the hope of obtaining a new lease of existence elsewhere." And they do these things not because they are "weak" or "sinful" or merely out for a "good time."

> Most people get a fair amount of fun out of their lives, but on balance life is suffering, and only the very young or the very foolish imagine otherwise. Ultimately it is the Christian attitude which is self-interested and hedonistic, since the aim is always to get away from the painful struggle of

earthly life and find eternal peace in some kind of Heaven or Nirvana.[38]

Orwell illustrates this difference in his analysis of Tolstoy's dislike of Shakespeare's verbal "exuberance," which Orwell explains as a "tendency to take—not so much a pleasure as simply an interest in the actual process of life." In his last years, Orwell remarks, Tolstoy was like an old man irritated by the purposeless but not causeless jumping of a small child; the old man wonders why the child cannot "sit still" as he does. "In a way the old man is in the right, but the trouble is that the child has a feeling in its limbs which the old man has lost. And if the old man knows of the existence of this feeling, the effect is merely to increase his irritation: he would make children senile, if he could." [39] Just as the "priest of power" would kill desire, the Mrs. Creevy's of the earth would stifle curiosity, and the hangmen and commissars would arrest the turning of the globe to prevent the recurrent nuisance of spring, primroses, and publishing poets.

The "irrelevancies" of life are (as Orwell says Shakespeare's "irrelevancies" are) the "products of excessive vitality." And this vitality in excess of what is used up merely to stay alive is the essence of human life, a superfluity without which life itself is superfluous. It causes a *Tropic of Cancer* to be written when the sober world is worried about mere survival; it causes a middle-aged business man to marvel irrelevantly at the infinite variety of life in a drop of water; it causes the aspidistra to fly and the sunflower, rooted in one place, to follow the steps of the sun.

The ordinary human being, like Shakespeare, is not a "philosopher or a scientist" but he does have curiosity. He loves the "surface of the earth and the process of life," which, Orwell insists, "is *not* the same thing as wanting to have a good time and stay alive as long as possible." It is, more finely, an "esthetic enthusiasm" which characterizes those who love this earth and the world they inherit from men like themselves: fallible but declaring the dignity of their kind and the value of life simply by living it. There are some, for example, who like the artists love language and some who like hangmen suspect its seductive power. Happily seduced and certain that "the music of words is something that belongs to this world,"[40] Orwell declared that the "same issue" separated the humanist, who loved things of this world, and the saint, who abjured them.

Orwell maintained—although it hardly led him to "quietism"—a "belief amounting to mysticism" in the worth of human life. He was neither philosopher nor social scientist, but he justified the ways of Man to men and infallibly smelled out his natural enemies. His private mystique was bound up nostalgically with misty skies and suet puddings, rare bursts of northern sunlight on a green island, soot-covered workers' shacks, and the stubborn personal loyalties of people to each other and to the land they lived on. Such a mystique is possible only in the free world where private values withstand the temptation to avoid the pain of living. As an article of faith that can never be verified except by the way men choose to live, Orwell believed in innate commandments: men shall not, in the name of whatsoever god, tyrannize over their fellow men; they shall have work which dignifies them and privacy which restores them; they shall be true to each other in the absence of God exactly as though He were present. It is hard to match for poignancy in context the lyric that Orwell—who was such a miserable poet but such a successful parodist of bad verse—created for the moment of brief, indefinable remorse Winston Smith suffers when he has broken this last commandment:

> "Under the spreading chestnut tree
> I sold you and you sold me—"

Because Orwell believed it was natural for human beings to love each other rather than causes, he was the implacable enemy of ideologies which supplanted human loyalties. Paradoxically, the strongest political defense he devised against the monstrous totalitarian usurpers of "ownlife" is an irrational, almost mystical belief—one he attributes to the English: "a respect for constitutionalism and legality, the belief in 'the law' as something above the State and above the individual," which, however cruel or stupid its embodiment in particular laws at particular times, is held to be, in essence, *incorruptible*.[41]

Orwell would seem to have in mind here a transcendent idea of right and wrong, which is bred in the bone like the "Christian moral code." But constitutionalism, unlike the ideological mystique which relies for interpretation upon mere expedience or the caprice of a Leader, establishes communal purposes and, in particular laws, defines areas in which the individual *shall not be eccentric*—the extent to which he is "*not* altogether an individual." These laws are neither unalterable nor impossible to keep. The area not so defined is the inviolable area of personal freedom and moral choice.

In this respect for governments founded in law lies the dormant resistance to totalitarianism and the hope that life, liberty, and the *pursuit* of happiness—if never its final attainment—shall not perish from the face of the earth, the hope, perhaps, that "Oceania" will keep alive the "spirit of man" and act as a bridge between the past and the future.

NOTES

Chapter One

1. *Keep the Aspidistra Flying* (London: Secker and Warburg, 1954), p. 197.

2. "Why I Write," *The Orwell Reader* (New York: Harcourt, Brace and Company, 1956), p. 393.

3. "Charles Dickens," *Dickens, Dali and Others: Studies In Popular Culture* (New York: Reynal and Hitchcock, 1946), p. 56.

4. "Politics and the English Language," *Orwell Reader*, pp. 363–64.

5. "W. B. Yeats," *Dickens, Dali and Others*, p. 169.

6. "Why I Write," *Orwell Reader*, p. 394.

7. "Looking Back on the Spanish War," *Such, Such Were the Joys* (New York: Harcourt, Brace and Company, 1953), pp. 142–43.

8. "Writers and Leviathan," *Such, Such Were the Joys*, pp. 65–66.

9. *Ibid.*, p. 65.

10. "In Defence of P. G. Wodehouse," *Dickens, Dali and Others*, pp. 222–43, *passim.*

11. "W. B. Yeats," *Dickens, Dali and Others*, pp. 161–69, *passim.*

12. "Charles Dickens," *Dickens, Dali and Others*, p. 70.

13. *Ibid.*, pp. 22–23.

14. "Raffles and Miss Blandish," *Dickens, Dali and Others*, p. 219.

15. "Charles Dickens," *Dickens, Dali and Others*, p. 75.

16. "Raffles and Miss Blandish," *Dickens, Dali and Others*, pp. 216–17.

17. "Charles Dickens," *Dickens, Dali and Others*, p. 23.

18. *Homage to Catalonia* (New York: Harcourt, Brace and Company, 1952), p. 124.

19. "Raffles and Miss Blandish," *Dickens, Dali and Others*, p. 220.

20. "Decline of the English Murder," *Orwell Reader*, p. 383.

21. "Rudyard Kipling," *Dickens, Dali and Others*, p. 142.

22. "Writers and Leviathan," *Such, Such Were the Joys,* p. 72.

23. "Benefit of Clergy: Some Notes on Salvador Dali," *Dickens, Dali and Others,* p. 177.

24. *Ibid.,* pp. 178–79.

25. "Why I Write," *Orwell Reader,* p. 394.

26. *Ibid.,* p. 395. "Politics and the English Language," *Orwell Reader,* p. 362.

27. "Politics and the English Language," *Orwell Reader,* p. 363.

28. *Nineteen Eighty-Four* (New York: Harcourt, Brace and Company, 1949), pp. 54, 199.

29. "England Your England," *The Lion and the Unicorn: Socialism and the English Genius* (London: Secker and Warburg, 1962), pp. 38–40.

30. "Raffles and Miss Blandish," *Dickens, Dali and Others,* p. 218.

31. "Looking Back on the Spanish War," *Such, Such Were the Joys,* p. 133. See also *Homage to Catalonia,* p. 180: "every war suffers a kind of progessive degradation with every month that it continues, because such things as individual liberty and a truthful press are simply not compatible with military efficiency."

32. "England Your England," *The Lion and the Unicorn,* p. 38.

33. Uncritical patriotism was of course susceptible to evil as well as good courses. In *1984* even sophisticated Party members are easily manipulated by telescreen hypnosis in the Two-Minutes Hate: "the rage that one felt was an abstract, undirected emotion which could be switched from one object to another like the flame of a blowlamp." *1984,* p. 16.

34. "Looking Back on the Spanish War," *Such, Such Were the Joys,* p. 131.

35. "The Prevention of Literature," *Orwell Reader,* p. 374.

36. *Homage to Catalonia,* pp. 46 ff.

37. "Looking Back on the Spanish War," *Such, Such Were the Joys,* p. 150.

38. *Homage to Catalonia,* p. 104.

39. *Ibid.,* p. 57.

40. "The Prevention of Literature," *Orwell Reader,* p. 370.

41. "Looking Back on the Spanish War," *Such, Such Were the Joys,* p. 146—although he was to imagine such wars in *1984.*

42. *Ibid.,* p. 132.

43. *Ibid.,* pp. 139–41.

44. "The Prevention of Literature," *Orwell Reader,* p. 371.

45. "Looking Back on the Spanish War," *Such, Such Were the Joys,* pp. 141–42.

46. "The Prevention of Literature," *Orwell Reader,* p. 371.

47. "Looking Back on the Spanish War," *Such, Such Were the Joys,* p. 148.

48. "Shooting an Elephant," *Orwell Reader,* p. 4.

49. "Rudyard Kipling," *Dickens, Dali and Others,* p. 145.

50. *Keep the Aspidistra Flying,* p. 122.

51. *Ibid.,* p. 110.

52. *Ibid.,* p. 55.

53. "The English Revolution," *The Lion and the Unicorn,* p. 72.

54. "Politics and the English Language," *Orwell Reader,* p. 364.

55. "Inside the Whale," *Such, Such Were the Joys,* pp. 197, 188.

56. *Ibid.,* pp. 155–56.

57. *Ibid.,* pp. 181–91, passim.

58. *Ibid.,* p. 156.

59. *Ibid.,* pp. 192, 194.

60. *Ibid.,* pp. 164–65.

61. *Ibid.,* pp. 196, 198.

62. "Politics vs. Literature," *Orwell Reader,* pp. 297–300.

63. "The Prevention of Literature," *Orwell Reader,* p. 376.

64. *Ibid.,* p. 373.

65. *Ibid.,* p. 373.

66. *Ibid.,* p. 374.

67. *Ibid.,* p. 379.

68. "Writers and Leviathan," *Such, Such Were the Joys,* p. 72.

69. "The Prevention of Literature," *Orwell Reader,* pp. 374–77.

70. "Writers and Leviathan," *Such, Such Were the Joys,* pp. 66–71.

71. *Ibid.,* pp. 67–70.

Chapter Two

1. *Keep the Aspidistra Flying,* pp. 69, 63, 73.

2. *Homage to Catalonia,* pp. 187.

3. "Why I Write," *Orwell Reader,* p. 394.

4. *Coming up for Air* (London: Secker and Warburg, 1959), p. 110.

5. See particularly Orwell's sensitive description of the industrial towns of England in *The Road to Wigan Pier.*

6. *Down and Out in Paris and London,* (New York: Harcourt, Brace and Company, 1950), pp. 201–5, *passim.*

7. *Ibid.,* pp. 203, 19.

8. *Ibid.,* p. 204.

9. *Keep the Aspidistra Flying,* p. 15.

10. *Down and Out in Paris and London,* p. 119.

11. Orwell suggests in *The Road to Wigan Pier* (New York: Harcourt, Brace and Company, 1958), pp. 70–73, that dirt may be indispensable to human happiness and "eternal dirt" rather than "eternal vigilance" the price of liberty. Despite the squalor and disrepair of the hovels in which English laborers lived, he found that they were humanly preferable to the aseptic, company-sponsored housing developments. He proves he is as conscience-ridden as any Anglo-Saxon when he decides, after a struggle with his instinct, in favor of clean, efficient new apartment houses rising on the rubble of the slums.

12. *Down and Out in Paris and London,* p. 20.

13. *Keep the Aspidistra Flying,* p. 57.

14. Joseph Conrad, *Lord Jim* (Boston: Houghton Mifflin Company, 1958), p. 141.

15 "Looking Back on the Spanish War," *Such, Such Were the Joys,* pp. 143–44.

16. *1984,* pp. 72, 91.

17. "No job is more fascinating than teaching if you have a free hand at it"—although, as Dorothy discovers, "that 'if' is one of the biggest 'ifs' in the world."—*A Clergyman's Daughter* (New York: Harcourt, Brace and Company, 1960), p. 244.

18. *Ibid.,* p. 135.

19. *Ibid.,* p. 202.

20. *1984,* p. 184.

21. *Ibid.,* p. 25.

22. *Coming up for Air,* p. 14.

23. "England Your England," *The Lion and the Unicorn,* pp. 13–14. In *The Road to Wigan Pier,* pp. 148–50, there is a comforting, almost sentimental, description of happy family life around the hearth of a worker who has steady, if not very remunerative, employment.

24. *Keep the Aspidistra Flying,* p. 57. See also *Down and Out in Paris and London,* pp. 17–18.

25. *Keep the Aspidistra Flying,* p. 23.

26. *Ibid.,* pp. 268–69.

27. *Ibid.,* p. 15.

28. *Ibid.*, p. 128.

29. *Ibid.*, p. 129.

30. *Ibid.*, p. 291.

31. *Ibid.*, pp. 302–3.

32. *1984*, p. 207.

33. *Ibid.*, pp. 191–92.

34. *Ibid.*, p. 191.

35. "Looking Back on the Spanish War," *Such, Such Were the Joys*, p. 151.

36. *The Road to Wigan Pier*, p. 209.

37. *Ibid.*, p. 193.

38. *Ibid.*, p. 200.

39. *Ibid.*, p. 226.

40. *Ibid.*, p. 240.

41. Napoleon, the Stalin of *Animal Farm*, is eventually denominated "Father of All Animals, Terror of Mankind, Protector of the Sheep-fold, Ducklings' Friend, and the like"—epithets matched only by those of the Emperor of Lilliput himself, whose custom it was, "after the Court had decreed any cruel Execution, either to gratify the Monarch's Resentment, or the Malice of a Favourite," to publicize "his *great Lenity and Tenderness, as Qualities known and confessed by all the World.*" Nothing, Gulliver reports, terrified "the People so much as those Encomiums on his Majesty's Mercy; because it was observed, that the more these Praises were enlarged and insisted on, the more *inhuman* was the Punishment, and the *Sufferer more innocent.*" In his examination of *Gulliver's Travels*, Orwell commends as Swift's "greatest contribution to political thought" his prevision of and attack upon "what would now be called totalitarianism." ("Politics vs. Literature," *Orwell Reader*, p. 290.)

42. *The Road to Wigan Pier*, p. 50.

43. *Ibid.*, p. 229.

44. "I Write As I Please," *Orwell Reader*, pp. 385–88.

45. "The English Revolution," *The Lion and the Unicorn*, pp. 76–77.

46. Hannah Arendt makes the horrifying functional aspect of such a society succinctly clear in "Franz Kafka: A Revaluation," *Partisan Review*, Fall, 1944. The full development and implications of this concept may be found in *The Human Condition*, published originally by the University of Chicago Press in 1958 and easily accessible in the Doubleday Anchor Books edition of 1959. The reader conversant with the range of Dr. Arendt's work will not need to be told the extent to which I am indebted to it for a clarification and formulation of the problems which particularly tantalized and disturbed Orwell.

Chapter Three

1. *Animal Farm* (New York: Harcourt, Brace and Company, 1946), p. 10.

2. *1984,* p. 192.

3. "Reflection on Gandhi," *Orwell Reader,* p. 332.

4. A martyrdom, to be meaningful, must be witnessed. The "locked loneliness" in which Party members live makes gestures of defiance almost inconceivable. Everyone is, by *being human,* martyred in advance of having lived or acted. The "murder of the moral person in man" is accomplished under totalitarianism, Hannah Arendt says, "by making martyrdom, for the first time in history, impossible." *The Origins of Totalitarianism* (New York: Meridian Books, Inc., 1958), p. 451.

5. *1984,* pp. 257–58.

6. *Ibid.,* p. 264. An illuminating study of the similarity of attaining Nirvana, of attaining adjustment through psychoanalysis, and of attaining orthodoxy through brainwashing can be found in Ernest Becker's *Zen: A Rational Critique* (New York: W. W. Norton and Company, Inc., 1961).

7. *The Road to Wigan Pier,* p. 160.

8. *1984,* p. 102.

9. *Ibid.,* pp. 242–43.

10. *Homage to Catalonia,* p. 212.

11. "Looking Back on the Spanish War," *Such, Such Were the Joys,* pp. 135–36.

12. "Shooting an Elephant," *Orwell Reader,* pp. 6–7. Flory makes the same struggle in *Burmese Days.*

13. "England Your England," *The Lion and the Unicorn,* pp. 15–18.

14. "Such, such were the joys . . .", *Such, Such Were the Joys,* p. 61.

15. Joseph Conrad, *Lord Jim,* p. 243.

16. *Ibid.,* p. 34.

17. *Ibid.,* p. 39.

18. *Ibid.,* p. 243.

19. *Ibid.,* p. 51.

20. *Ibid.,* p. 160.

21. *Ibid.,* p. 38.

22. "England Your England," *The Lion and the Unicorn,* pp. 28–29.

23. *Homage to Catalonia,* p. 45.

24. *Ibid.*, pp. 195–211, *passim.*

25. *Ibid.*, p. 232.

26. *Keep the Aspidistra Flying,* p. 293.

27. "Looking Back on the Spanish War," *Such, Such Were the Joys,* pp. 151–52.

28. "England Your England," *The Lion and the Unicorn,* pp. 27–28.

29. "The Art of Donald McGill," *Dickens, Dali and Others,* p. 137.

30. "England Your England," *The Lion and the Unicorn,* pp. 44, 20–21.

31. "Notes on Nationalism," *Such, Such Were the Joys,* p. 74.

32. *Coming Up for Air,* pp. 106–10, *passim.*

33. *Ibid.*, p. 152.

34. *Ibid.*, p. 163. I would not be American without mentioning Orwell's refusal to regard America as a bulwark against the gorilla hordes, occidental or oriental. He seems to have hated America for her latter-day barbarism in commerce and crime too strongly either to respect her constitutional government or admit her prowess in the struggle against totalitarianism. Beyond the tiny western corner of Great Britain, the world fell off—at least until Orwell's rediscovery of America in 1942.

35. *Ibid.*, pp. 227–29.

36. "England Your England," *The Lion and the Unicorn,* p. 14.

37. "Charles Dickens," *Dickens, Dali and Others,* p. 74.

38. *1984,* pp. 220–21.

39. *Ibid.*, pp. 273–76.

40. "Shopkeepers at War," *The Lion and the Unicorn,* pp. 47–48.

41. *Ibid.*, p. 63.

42. "Notes on Nationalism," *Such, Such Were the Joys,* pp. 90, 95.

43. "Reflections on Gandhi," *Orwell Reader,* p. 334.

44. *The Road to Wigan Pier,* pp. 190–92.

45. "Arthur Koestler," *Dickens, Dali and Others,* pp. 199–200.

46. *Ibid.*, pp. 187–89.

47. "Wells, Hitler and the World State," *Dickens, Dali and Others,* p. 120.

48. *Ibid.*, p. 118.

49. *The Road to Wigan Pier,* p. 177.

50. *1984,* p. 230. Describing the concentration camps of totalitarian systems, Hannah Arendt writes, "The criminals everywhere constitute the aristocracy of the camps." *The Origins of Totalitarianism,* p. 448.

51. Arendt, *The Origins of Totalitarianism,* p. 448.

52. "Arthur Koestler," *Dickens, Dali and Others,* pp. 187, 191.

53. *The Road to Wigan Pier,* pp. 178–79.

54. Arendt, *The Origins of Totalitarianism,* pp. 470–71.

55. "The Prevention of Literature," *Orwell Reader,* p. 371.

56. Arendt, *The Origins of Totalitarianism,* p. 459. The self-destructiveness inherent in totalitarian systems received prophetic attention from Hermann Broch on the eve, figuratively, of Hitler's eruption in Germany. In his trilogy *The Sleepwalkers* (available translated from the German by Willa and Edwin Muir in the Universal Library edition published by Grosser & Dunlap in 1964) Broch reasons as follows: ". . . when people say that 'a man without feelings is no man at all,' they say so out of some perception of the truth that no system of values can exist without an irreducible residue of the irrational which preserves the rational itself from a literally suicidal autonomy, from a 'super rationality' that is, if anything, still more objectionable, still more 'evil' and 'sinful' from the standpoint of the value-system, than the irrational: for, in contradistinction to the plastic irrational, the pure Ratio, arising through dialectic and deduction, becomes set and incapable of further formation when it grows autonomous, and this rigidity annuls its own logicality and brings it up against its logical limit of infinity,—when reason becomes autonomous it is thus radically evil, for in annulling the logicality of the value-system it destroys the system itself. . . ," pp. 626–27.

57. "The Prevention of Literature," *Orwell Reader,* pp. 371–72.

58. Like Orwell, Robinson Jeffers was averse to notions of perfectibility and stoically committed to a choice of evils. For Jeffers the ugliest factions —to say nothing of the "least ugly faction" (the phrase appears in his poem "The Answer")—become part of a "divinely superfluous beauty," Orwell would probably have dismissed him as a "yogi"—his contemptuous label for death-worshipers, for those who long to resign what Jeffers calls "rankling consciousness."

59. *1984,* pp. 217–18.

60. *Ibid.,* p. 268.

61. *Ibid.,* p. 81.

Chapter Four

1. Samuel Johnson, *The History of Rasselas, Prince of Abyssinia,* chap. ii.

2. *A Clergyman's Daughter,* p. 281.

3. *Ibid.,* pp. 278–79.

4. *Ibid.,* p. 269.

5. *Ibid.,* p. 278.

6. *Ibid.*, p. 315.

7. *Ibid.*, p. 308.

8. *Ibid.*, p. 315. Writing of Swift's "diseased" vision in *Gulliver's Travels,* Orwell says: "Part of our minds—in any normal person it is the dominant part—believes that man is a noble animal and life is worth living: but there is also an inner self which at least intermittently stands aghast at the horror of existence." In "his endless harping on disease, dirt, and deformity," Swift appeals to our subjective reaction to horror and pain, both of which we know are "necessary to the continuance of life on this planet." If they are, the pessimist reasons that life cannot be "significantly improved." Swift's attitude "is in effect the Christian attitude, minus the bribe of a 'next world'—which, however probably has less hold upon the minds of believers than the conviction that this world is a vale of tears and the grave is a place of rest. It is, I am certain, a wrong attitude, and one which could have harmful effects upon behavior; but something in us responds to it. . . ." ("Politics vs. Literature," *Orwell Reader,* p. 299.)

9. *A Clergyman's Daughter,* p. 316.

10. *Ibid.*, p. 317.

11. Thomas Carlyle, "The Everlasting Yea," *Sartor Resartus.*

12. Hannah Arendt, *Between Past and Future* (New York: The Viking Press, 1961), pp. 146–47.

13. "The Prevention of Literature," *Orwell Reader,* p. 374.

14. *1984,* pp. 205, 73.

15. *Ibid.*, p. 60.

16. *Ibid.*, p. 234.

17. "Such, such were the joys . . .", *Such, Such Were the Joys,* p. 13.

18. *Ibid.*, p. 16.

19. *Ibid.*, pp. 21–28.

20. *1984,* p. 213.

21. "Such, such were the joys . . .", *Such, Such Were the Joys,* p. 29.

22. "The Prevention of Literature," *Orwell Reader,* p. 373.

23. "Such, such were the joys . . .", *Such, Such Were the Joys,* p. 30.

24. *Ibid.*, p. 35.

25. *Ibid.*, p. 39.

26. *Ibid.*, pp. 54–55.

27. "England Your England," *The Lion and the Unicorn,* p. 14.

28. "Such, such were the joys . . .", *Such, Such Were the Joys,* p. 62.

29. *1984,* p. 207.

30. *Ibid.,* p. 211.

31. *Ibid.,* pp. 265–67.

32. *Ibid.,* p. 270.

33. During the period of gestation for *1984,* Orwell complained that the "Catholic and the Communist are alike in assuming that an opponent cannot be both honest and intelligent. Each of them tacitly claims that 'the truth' has already been revealed, and that the heretic, if he is not simply a fool, is secretly aware of 'the truth' and merely resists it out of selfish motives," ("The Prevention of Literature," *Orwell Reader,* p. 369.)

34. *1984,* p. 261.

35. *Ibid., p.* 281.

36. *Ibid.,* pp. 283–84.

37. *Ibid.,* p. 287.

38. *Ibid.,* p. 256.

39. *Homage to Catalonia,* p. 104.

40. "A Hanging," *Orwell Reader,* pp. 10–11.

41. "Lear, Tolstoi and the Fool," *Orwell Reader,* p. 306.

Chapter Five

1. *A Clergyman's Daughter,* p. 16.

2. *Burmese Days* (London: Secker and Warburg, 1949), p. 57.

3. *Coming Up for Air,* pp. 167, 177.

4. Orwell quotes the poem from which this comes in "Why I Write."

5. William Blake, "The Divine Image."

6. Hannah Arendt, *The Human Condition,* p. 283.

7. *1984,* pp. 65–66.

8. *Ibid.,* p. 134.

9. *Keep the Aspidistra Flying,* p. 123.

10. John Donne, "The Good-morrow."

11. *1984,* p. 148.

12. Thomas Hardy, "The Darkling Thrush."

13. *1984,* p. 165.

14. *Keep the Aspidistra Flying,* p. 127.

15. *1984,* p. 137.

16. *Ibid.,* pp. 124–27.

17. *A Clergyman's Daughter,* p. 294.
18. *The Road to Wigan Pier,* pp. 19, 150.
19. "Arthur Koestler," *Dickens, Dali and Others,* p. 189.
20. William Blake, "The Little Girl Lost."
21. Hannah Arendt, *Between Past and Future,* p. 156.

Chapter Six

1. "Second Thoughts on James Burnham," *Orwell Reader,* p. 352.
2. "Lear, Tolstoi and the Fool," *Ibid.,* p. 314.
3. *Coming Up for Air,* p. 167, 177.
4. "Lear, Tolstoi and the Fool,"*Orwell Reader,* p. 314.
5. "Notes on Nationalism," *Such, Such Were the Joys,* pp. 82–83.
6. *Ibid.,* pp. 85–86.
7. *Ibid.,* pp. 93–94.
8. *Ibid.,* p. 96.
9. *Ibid.,* p. 97.
10. "The English Revolution," *The Lion and the Unicorn,* p. 85.
11. "Second Thoughts on James Burnham," *Orwell Reader,* p. 347.
12. *Ibid.,* p. 347.
13. *Ibid.,* p. 348.
14. *Ibid.,* pp. 349–50.
15. *Ibid.,* pp. 352, 354.
16. "Politics vs. Literature," *Orwell Reader,* p. 300.
17. "Arthur Koestler," *Dickens, Dali and Others,* pp. 191, 201.
18. "The English Revolution," *The Lion and the Unicorn,* p. 95.
19. *Ibid.,* p. 96.
20. *Ibid.,* p. 74.
21. *Ibid.,* p. 75.
22. *Ibid.,* p. 88.
23. *Ibid.,* p. 86.
24. *Ibid.,* pp. 91–92.
25. *Ibid.,* p. 94.
26. *Ibid.,* p. 93.
27. "Arthur Koestler," *Dickens, Dali and Others,* p. 190.
28. *Ibid.,* pp. 200–201.

29. *Ibid.*, p. 189.

30. George Woodcock, *The Crystal Spirit, A Study of George Orwell* (Boston: Little, Brown and Company, 1966), pp. 310–11.

31. "Politics vs. Literature," *Orwell Reader*, pp. 292–94.

32. *Ibid.*, p. 293.

33. *Ibid.*, p. 294.

34. *Ibid.*, pp. 294–95.

35. *Ibid.*, p. 296.

36. *Ibid.*, pp. 296–97.

37. "Lear, Tolstoi and the Fool," *Orwell Reader*, p. 312.

38. *Ibid.*, p. 312.

39. *Ibid.*, p. 307.

40. *Ibid.*, pp. 313–14.

41. "England Your England," *The Lion and the Unicorn*, p. 19.

INDEX